Testing and Management Handbook

Level 6

Siegfried Engelmann
Jean Osborn
Steve Osborn
Leslie Zoref

A Division of The McGraw-Hill Companies

Columbus, Ohio

www.sra4kids.com

SRA/McGraw-Hill

A Division of The McGraw·Hill Companies

Send all inquiries to:
SRA/McGraw-Hill
8787 Orion Place
Columbus, OH 43240-4027

Printed in the United States of America.

ISBN 0-07-569182-5

2 3 4 5 6 7 8 9 DBH 06 05 04 03 02

Reading Mastery Plus

SRA

Plus

Testing and Management Handbook

Level 6

Siegfried Engelmann
Jean Osborn
Steve Osborn
Leslie Zoref

A Division of The McGraw·Hill Companies

Columbus, Ohio

Introduction

The testing and management system for *Reading Mastery Plus,* Level 6, is a complete system for monitoring student performance in the program. By using the testing and management system, you can

- ensure that students are properly placed in the program
- measure student achievement within the program
- identify the skills and concepts the students have mastered
- maintain individual and group records
- administer remedial exercises

This handbook contains all the materials for the testing and management system. Included here are instructions for administering the tests and remedial exercises for each test. Blackline masters in this Handbook include a placement test, twelve mastery tests, twelve writing prompts (for optional use with the mastery tests), an Individual Skills Profile Chart, a Group Point Chart, and a Writing Assessment Chart.

The Tests

Two kinds of tests are used in the testing and management system: the placement test and the mastery tests. The placement test appears on page 74. It measures the decoding and comprehension skills of students entering *Reading Mastery Plus,* Level 6. The test results provide guidelines for grouping students and allow you to identify students who should not be placed in the program.

The mastery tests are criterion referenced, which means they test each student's achievement within the program. Each test item measures student mastery of a specific skill or concept taught in *Reading Mastery Plus,* Level 6. There are twelve mastery tests, one for every ten lessons. The tests for lessons 30, 60, 90, and 120 are unit tests measuring mastery of skills and concepts taught in the preceding thirty lessons.

For each mastery test, a writing prompt is included as an optional test item. You may have students begin the writing test item while they wait for others to finish the mastery test, or you may have students complete it at another time. Writing test items begin on page 119. Evaluation guidelines for writing items begin on page 131.

The Charts

Three charts are used in the testing and management system: the Individual Skills Profile Chart, the Group Point Chart, and the Writing Assessment Chart. The Individual Skills Profile Chart appears on pages 68 and 69. This two-page chart lists the specific skills and concepts taught in *Reading Mastery Plus,* Level 6, and indicates what each test item measures. When the chart is completed, it will show how well a student has mastered the skills and concepts taught in *Reading Mastery Plus,* Level 6.

The Group Point Chart appears on pages 71 and 72. It summarizes the group's scores on the mastery tests. The chart provides an objective measure of the group's progress and can be used to evaluate the group's overall performance.

The Writing Assessment Chart on page 73 provides a form on which students can keep a record of their scores on the writing test items.

The Remedial Exercises

To pass each mastery test, a student must answer at least 80 percent of the items correctly. The remedial exercises are designed to help students who score below 80 percent on the mastery tests. Each test has its own set of remedial exercises. The exercises provide a general review of the tested skills and concepts, using examples different from those on the test. There is a specific remedial exercise for every tested skill or concept. The remedial exercises are similar to the exercises found in the Presentation Books for *Reading Mastery Plus,* Level 6.

Use of Color, Bold, and Italic Type

Text is distinguished in the following ways for your convenience in administering the test and presenting remedial exercises.

- Blue text shows what you say.
- **Bold blue text shows words you stress.**

- (Text in parentheses tells what you do.)
- *Italic text gives students' responses.* (If a student response is preceded by the word *Response,* the printed response gives the exact answer expected. If a student response is preceded by the word *Idea,* the printed response gives the general idea of a correct answer.)

The Placement Test

The placement test has two parts. In part 1, each student reads a passage aloud as you count decoding errors. In part 2, students answer comprehension questions about the passage.

Instructions for Part 1

You should administer part 1 in a corner of the classroom so that other students will not overhear the testing. Use the following procedure.

1. (Give the student a copy of the placement test.)
2. (Point to the passage and say:) You're going to read the passage aloud. I want you to read it as well as you can. Don't try to read it so fast you make mistakes, but don't read it so slowly that it doesn't make any sense. You have two minutes to read the passage. Go.
3. (Time the student and make one tally mark for each error.)
4. (After two minutes, stop the student. Count every word not read as an error.)
5. (Total the student's errors.)

Use the following guidelines in counting decoding errors for part 1.

- If the student misreads a word, count one error.
- If the student omits a word ending, such as *s* or *ed,* count one error.
- If the student reads a word incorrectly and then correctly, count one error.
- If the student sounds out a word instead of reading it normally, count one error.
- If the student does not identify a word within three seconds, tell the student the word and count one error.
- If the student skips a word, count one error.
- If the student skips a line, point to the line and count one error.
- If the student does not finish the passage within the given time limit, count every word not read as an error. For example, if the student is eight words from the end of the passage at the end of the time limit, count eight errors.

Instructions for Part 2

After all the students have finished part 1, administer part 2 to the entire group. Use the following procedure.

1. (Assemble the students.)
2. (Give each student a copy of the placement test.)
3. (Say:) Here is the passage you read earlier. Read the passage again silently; then answer the questions in part 2. You have seven minutes. Go.
4. (Collect the test papers after seven minutes.)
5. (Total each student's errors, using the answer key below.)

Answer Key for Part 2

1. Response: *A king.*
2. Response: *A princess.*
3. Ideas: *His daughter; Marygold.*
4. Response: *Gold.*
5. Ideas: *His daughter; gold.*
6. Idea: *They weren't gold.*
7. Response: *Roses.*
8. Response: *Perfume.*
9. Idea: *How much it would be worth if the roses were gold.*

Placement Guidelines

Place your students as follows:

- Students who made zero to six errors on part 1 *and* zero to two errors on part 2 can be placed in *Reading Mastery Plus,* Level 6.
- Students who made more than six errors on part 1 or more than two errors on part 2 should be given the placement test for *Reading Mastery Plus,* Level 5.

Lesson 10

Administering the Test

The Lesson 10 Mastery Test should be administered after the students complete all work on lesson 10 and before they begin work on lesson 11. Each student will need a pencil and a copy of the test. Use the following script.

1. (Have the students clear their desks. Make sure each student has a pencil.)
2. Now you're going to take a short test on what you've learned. I'll give each of you a copy of the test. Don't begin until I tell you. (Pass out the tests.)
3. Write your name on the name line in the upper right-hand corner of each page.
4. Look at the sample items. I'll read the first sample item.
   For item 1, circle the letter of the answer that means the same thing as the underlined part.
   1. Several cows were grazing in the pasture.
      a. eating plants
      b. running around
      c. sleeping
5. What is the correct answer? (Response: *Eating plants.*)
   • Everybody, circle the letter for that answer.
   • What letter did you circle? (Response: *A.*)
6. I'll read the next sample item.
   For item 2, circle the letter of the correct answer.
   2. What was the name of Homer's uncle?
      a. Odysseus
      b. Ulysses
      c. Mr. Gabby
7. What is the correct answer? (Response: *Ulysses.*)
   • Everybody, circle the letter for that answer.
   • What letter did you circle? (Response: *B.*)
   (Make sure all students have circled the letters correctly.)

8. You will answer all the items on the test just as you answered these sample items. For some items, you must circle the letter of the answer that means the same thing as the underlined part. For other items, you must circle the letter of the correct answer.
9. Now you're ready to begin the test. Answer all the items on both pages. For each item, you must circle the letter of the correct answer. There is no time limit. When you've finished, turn your test facedown and look up at me. Begin the test now. (If you are including the writing item as part of the testing session, tell students they can begin the writing item after they finish the mastery test.)

Grading the Test

You can grade the tests yourself, or you can have the students grade one another's tests. If you want the students to grade one another's tests, tell them to trade test papers. Then use the following procedure.

1. Now we're going to grade the test. I'll read the correct answer for each item. If the answer is correct, mark it with a **C**. If the answer is wrong, mark it with an **X**.
2. (Read the correct answers from the answer key on page 6.)
3. Now count the number of **correct** answers and enter the score at the end of the test.

Answer Key

Lesson 10

Sample Items

1. Several cows were grazing in the pasture.
   - a. eating plants
   - b. running around
   - c. sleeping

2. What was the name of Homer's uncle?
   - a. Odysseus
   - b. Ulysses
   - c. Mr. Gabby

For items 1–6, circle the letter of the answer that means the same thing as the underlined part.

1. The auto accident was a great misfortune.
   - a. calamity
   - b. mist
   - c. peril

2. No one died during the big earthquake.
   - a. enlarged
   - b. cherished
   - c. perished

3. The boy was suspicious of the free offer.
   - a. advanced
   - b. hideous
   - c. skeptical

4. The can opener is a useful gadget.
   - a. weapon
   - b. device
   - c. metal

5. The roaring elephants made a commotion at the zoo.
   - a. rodeo
   - b. sculpture
   - c. disturbance

6. The traveler encountered a dog and began to pet it.
   - a. came into contact with
   - b. followed closely
   - c. chased

For items 7–16, circle the letter of the correct answer.

7. What was the name of Odysseus's son?
   - a. Hermes
   - b. Telemachus
   - c. Polyphemus

Read the passage below. Then answer items 8–10.

People had begun to gather outside the lunch room window, and someone was saying, "There are almost as many doughnuts as there are people in Centerburg, and I wonder how in tarnation Ulysses thinks he can sell all of 'em!"

Every once in a while somebody would come inside and buy some, but while somebody bought two to eat and a dozen to take home, the machine made three dozen more.

By the time Uncle Ulysses and the sheriff arrived and pushed through the crowd, the lunch room was a calamity of doughnuts!

8. How did the people know there were a lot of doughnuts?
   - a. They heard about the doughnuts from the sheriff.
   - b. They saw the sandwich sign man.
   - c. They saw the doughnuts through the lunch room window.

Lesson 10 Test   75

9. Why did the author call the lunch room "a calamity of doughnuts"?
   - a. The machine made doughnuts faster than people bought them.
   - b. The doughnuts were stacked too high.
   - c. The sheriff didn't like doughnuts.

10. How could Uncle Ulysses solve the problem of too many doughnuts?
    - a. Have a doughnut sale
    - b. Open the window
    - c. Close the store

Read the passage below. Then answer items 11–16.

To their joy, as Odysseus and his crew left Circe's island, a strong wind blew from the north, driving the ship south. Presently the wind fell, and the sea was calm. Nearby, they saw a beautiful island from which came the sound of sweet singing. Odysseus knew who the singers were, for Circe had told him. They were the Sirens—beautiful mermaids who were deadly to men. The Sirens sat and sang among the flowers, but the flowers hid the bones of men who had listened to their singing. The singing had enchanted these men and carried their souls away. They had landed on the island and died of that strange music.

Odysseus wanted to hear the Sirens. He took a great piece of wax and cut it up into small pieces, which he gave to his men. Then he ordered his men to bind him tightly to the mast with ropes and told them not to unbind him until after they had passed the Sirens.

After Odysseus was bound to the mast, he ordered his men to soften the wax and place it in their ears so they would not hear the Sirens. When all this was done, the men sat down on the benches and pulled their oars. The ship rushed along and soon came near the island.

Odysseus heard the sweet singing of the Sirens. They seemed to offer him all knowledge and wisdom, which they knew he loved more than anything else in the world. He wanted to go to their island, and he begged his men to loosen his ropes. But the men could not hear him, and they rowed the ship past the island until the song of the Sirens faded away. Then they set Odysseus free and took the wax out of their ears.

11. Why couldn't the men hear the Sirens?
    - a. They were too far away.
    - b. They had wax in their ears.
    - c. The ocean made too much noise.

12. Why didn't Odysseus swim toward the Sirens?
    - a. He had wax in his ears.
    - b. His feet were in chains.
    - c. He was tied to the mast.

13. Why did Odysseus like the Sirens so much?
    - a. They seemed to offer him knowledge and wisdom.
    - b. They were the most beautiful creatures he had ever seen.
    - c. They carried his soul away to a beautiful place.

14. What was the first thing Odysseus ordered his men to do?
    - a. Put wax in their ears
    - b. Bind him to the mast
    - c. Loosen his ropes

15. What did the flowers hide?
    - a. The Sirens' tails
    - b. Deadly plants
    - c. The bones of men

16. In which place would you find rotting clothes?
    - a. Circe's island
    - b. The Sirens' island
    - c. Odysseus's boat

STOP – end of test – SCORE: _____

76   Reading Mastery Plus, Level 6

Recording Individual Results

The students record their test results on the Individual Skills Profile Chart. Use the following procedures to explain the chart.

1. (Give each student a copy of the appropriate chart. Tell the students to write their names on the name line at the upper right.)

2. This is your Individual Skills Profile Chart. Look at the left side of the chart. The words on the left side tell about the reading skills you're learning.

3. Look at the top line of the chart. The numbers on the top line are lesson numbers.
   - What is the first number? (Response: *10.*)
   - What is the last number? (Response: *60.*)

   You will take a test for each of the lesson numbers. When we finish lesson 60, I'll give you another sheet with numbers for lessons 70 through 120. You have just finished the test for lesson 10.

4. Now look at the column of numbers under lesson 10. Those numbers tell about the items on the test for lesson 10.
   - What is the first number in the column? (Response: *1.*)
   - That number tells about test item number 1. Now look **down** the column.
   - What is the last number in the column? (Response: *16.*)
   - What test item does that number tell about? (Response: *Item 16.*)

   You can see that the order of the numbers is not the same in every column.

5. Now I'll tell you how to record your test results on the chart. First, look at the test to find out which items you got wrong. Then circle those numbers on the chart.
   - Which number would you circle if you got number 2 wrong? (Response: *2.*)

6. Now record your results. I'll help you if you have questions. (**Circulate among the students as they record their results.**)

7. (After the students finish, say:) Now count the items you did **not** circle and write the total in the **Total** box near the bottom of the column. The total should be the same as your test score.

8. Below the **Total** box is the **Retest** box. If you scored zero to 12 points, write an **X** in the **Retest** box.

    Below the **Retest** box is the **FINAL SCORE** box. If you scored 13 to 16 points, write your score in the **FINAL SCORE** box.

Remedial Exercises

Students who scored 0 to 12 points on the test should be given remedial help. After the regular reading period is over, assemble these students and present the following exercises. The students will need their original test papers.

EXERCISE 1 Vocabulary Review

1. Let's talk about the meanings of some words.

2. The first word is **calamity. Calamity** is another word for **misfortune.**
    - Everybody, what's another way of saying **The man suffered many misfortunes**? (Signal.) *The man suffered many calamities.*

3. The next word is **mist.** A **mist** is a fine rain.
    - Everybody, what's another way of saying **She was walking in the fine rain**? (Signal.) *She was walking in the mist.*

4. The next word is **peril. Peril** is another word for **danger.**
    - Everybody, what's another way of saying **The traveler encountered danger**? (Signal.) *The traveler encountered peril.*

5. The next word is **enlarged.** When you **enlarge** something, you make it bigger.
    - Everybody, what's another way of saying **We made the room bigger**? (Signal.) *We enlarged the room.*

6. The next word is **cherish.** When you **cherish** something, you value it.
    - Everybody, what's another way of saying **The boy valued his dog**? (Signal.) *The boy cherished his dog.*

7. The next word is **perish.** When something **perishes,** it dies.
    - Everybody, what's another way of saying **The old cow died**? (Signal.) *The old cow perished.*

8. The next word is **advanced.** When something is **advanced,** it is **ahead of** other things.
    - Everybody, what's another way of saying **The scientist has ideas that are ahead of other people's ideas**? (Signal.) *The scientist has advanced ideas.*

9. The next word is **hideous.** When something is **hideous,** it is horrible or disgusting.
    - Everybody, what's another way of saying **The movie was about a disgusting monster**? (Signal.) *The movie was about a hideous monster.*

10. The next word is **skeptical.** When you are **skeptical** about something, you are suspicious of that thing.
    - Everybody, what's another way of saying **The woman was suspicious of the advertisement's promises**? (Signal.) *The woman was skeptical of the advertisement's promises.*

11. The next word is **gadget.** A **gadget** is a device.
    - Everybody, what's another way of saying **The girl used a special device to open the bottle**? (Signal.) *The girl used a special gadget to open the bottle.*

12. The next word is **commotion.** A **commotion** is a disturbance.
    - Everybody, what's another way of saying **The rock band created a disturbance**? (Signal.) *The rock band created a commotion.*

13. The last word is **encounter.** When you **encounter** something, you come into contact with that thing.
    - Everybody, what's another way of saying **They came into contact with a dragon**? (Signal.) *They encountered a dragon.*

EXERCISE 2   General Review

1. Who was Hermes? (Idea: *The messenger god.*)
   - Who was Telemachus? (Idea: *Odysseus's son.*)
   - Who was Polyphemus? (Idea: *A cyclops.*)

2. Everybody, look at the passage on page 76 of your test. We're going to figure out the main idea of the first paragraph. (Call on a student to read the first paragraph aloud. Correct any decoding errors.)

3. Who are the main characters in that paragraph? (Idea: *Odysseus and his men.*)
   - What is the main thing those characters do? (Idea: *Approach the Sirens.*)
   - So what is the main idea of the paragraph? (Idea: *Odysseus and his men approached the Sirens.*)

4. Name some supporting details for that main idea. (Ideas: *The men were headed north; they saw a beautiful island; they heard singing; Odysseus knew the singers were Sirens; the Sirens were mermaids.*)

EXERCISE 3   Passage Reading

1. Everybody, look at the passage on page 76 of your test. You're going to read the passage aloud.

2. (Call on individual students to read several sentences each. Correct any decoding errors. When the students finish, present the following questions.)

3. What did the men put into their ears? (Ideas: *Wax; pieces of wax.*)
   - With the wax in their ears, could they hear Odysseus beg? (Response: *No.*)

4. Why wasn't Odysseus able to move around the ship? (Idea: *He was tied to the mast.*)

5. What did Odysseus love more than anything else in the world? (Response: *Knowledge and wisdom.*)
   - Who seemed to offer Odysseus knowledge and wisdom? (Response: *The Sirens.*)

6. When did Odysseus order his men to place wax in their ears? (Idea: *After Odysseus was bound to the mast.*)

7. What happened to the men who had been enchanted by the Sirens? (Idea: *They had landed on the island and died.*)
   - How would the men change after they died? (Ideas: *Their clothes would rot; they would become skeletons.*)
   - What was hiding the skeletons of those men? (Idea: *Flowers.*)

Retesting the Students

After you've completed the remedial exercises, retest each student individually. To administer the retest, you will need the student's original test paper, a blank copy of the test, and a red pencil. Test the student in a corner of the classroom so that the other students will not overhear the testing. Give the student the blank copy of the test. Say, "Look at page 75. You're going to take this test again. Read each item aloud and tell me the answer."

Use the student's original test paper to grade the retest. Use the red pencil to mark each correct answer with a **C** and each incorrect answer with an **X**. Then count one point for each correct answer and write the new score at the bottom of the page. Finally, revise the Individual Skills Profile Chart by drawing an **X** over any items the student missed on the retest. The chart should now show which items the student missed on the initial test and which items the student missed on the retest.

Page 67 shows a partially completed Individual Skills Profile Chart.

Recording Group Results

After the students have completely filled in the Individual Skills Profile Chart for lesson 10, you should fill in the Group Point Chart, which appears on page 71. Make a copy of the chart and then enter the students' names on the left side of the chart under the heading "Names." Record the students' scores in the boxes under the appropriate lesson number. Record the students' final scores on the mastery test in the *right* side of each box. The left side is used for the individual reading checkouts, which are explained in the next section.

Page 70 shows a partially completed Group Point Chart.

Administering the Checkouts

The mastery test measures comprehension, literary appreciation, and study skills. Decoding skills are measured by the individual reading checkouts. For an individual reading checkout, a student reads a passage aloud as you count decoding errors. Students earn points for reading the passage accurately. A checkout takes about a minute and a half per student. Checkouts should be administered in a corner of the classroom so that the other students won't overhear.

The student will read a portion of the passage on page 76 of the test. This portion has been shaded on your answer key. Use the following procedure.

1. Tell the student to look at the passage on page 76 of the test.
2. Note the time and tell the student to begin reading the passage.
3. As the student reads, make a tally mark on a sheet of paper for each decoding error the student makes. (See page 4 for a complete description of decoding errors.)
4. At the end of one minute, tell the student to stop reading.
5. Award points as follows:
   0-2 errors – 2 points
   More than 2 errors – 0 points
6. Enter the student's score in the left side of the appropriate box on the Group Point Chart.

Tested Skills and Concepts

The Lesson 10 Mastery Test measures student mastery of the following skills and concepts.

- using vocabulary words in context (items 1–3)
- using context to predict word meaning (items 4–6)
- recalling details and events (item 7)
- inferring story details and events (item 8)
- drawing conclusions (item 9)
- evaluating problems and solutions (item 10)
- identifying literal cause and effect (item 11)
- inferring causes and effects (item 12)
- inferring a character's point of view (item 13)
- sequencing narrative events (item 14)
- answering literal questions about a text (item 15)
- distinguishing settings by features (item 16)

Lesson 20

Administering the Test

The Lesson 20 Mastery Test should be administered after the students complete all work on lesson 20 and before they begin work on lesson 21. Each student will need a pencil and a copy of the test. Use the following script.

1. (Have the students clear their desks. Make sure each student has a pencil.)
2. Now you're going to take another test on what you've learned. I'll give each of you a copy of the test. Don't begin until I tell you. (Pass out the tests.)
3. Write your name on the name line in the upper right-hand corner of each page.
4. Now you're ready to begin the test. Answer all the items on both pages. There is no time limit. When you've finished, turn your test facedown and look up at me. Begin the test now. (If you are including the writing item as part of the testing session, tell students they can begin the writing item after they finish the mastery test.)

Grading the Test

You can grade the tests yourself, or you can have the students grade one another's tests. If you want the students to grade one another's tests, tell them to trade test papers. Then use the following procedure.

1. Now we're going to grade the test. I'll read the correct answer for each item. If the answer is correct, mark it with a **C.** If the answer is wrong, mark it with an **X.**
2. (Read the correct answers from the answer key in the next column.)
3. Now count the number of **correct** answers and enter the score at the end of the test.

Answer Key

Lesson 20

Name _____

For items 1–6, circle the letter of the answer that means the same thing as the underlined part.

1. The details of the contract are his business.
   a. vow
   ⓑ affair
   c. spoil

2. The child smeared the carpet with her sticky fingers.
   ⓐ smudged
   b. neglected
   c. rotted

3. The young girl had a confused look on her face.
   a. courteous
   b. feeble
   ⓒ bewildered

4. The custom of removing our shoes soon became a habit.
   a. state law
   b. company rule
   ⓒ way of behaving

5. The burro was kept on a long rope.
   a. corn and beef casserole
   ⓑ small donkey
   c. brightly colored bird

6. The woman used a gourd to dig holes to plant seeds.
   ⓐ fruit with a hard shell
   b. tool with a wooden handle
   c. three-wheeled tractor

For items 7–16, circle the letter of the correct answer.

7. How did the beggar convince Penelope that he had really met Odysseus?
   ⓐ He told her what Odysseus wore.
   b. He told her about a birthmark Odysseus had.
   c. He told her a secret password.

8. How is a mesa different from a mountain?
   a. A mesa comes out of the ground.
   b. A mesa can be rocky.
   ⓒ A mesa has a flat top.

Read the paragraph below. Then answer items 9–10.

When the sides of the bowl were high enough, Grandmother took some dried pieces of gourd shell out of a basket. They were what she used for shaping the bowl. She took a piece that was curved just right and held it against the side of the bowl and pushed from inside, till it was shaped like the curve of the gourd.

9. What is the main idea of the paragraph?
   a. Grandmother used pieces of gourd shell.
   b. Grandmother took something out of a basket.
   ⓒ Grandmother shaped the bowl.

10. What is one supporting detail for that main idea?
   a. Grandmother lived on a mesa.
   b. Grandmother had a basket.
   ⓒ Grandmother pushed a gourd shell against the bowl.

Lesson 20 Test   77

Name _____

Read the passage below. Then answer items 11–16.

Mother and Father knew they would need money to buy food next winter. There are jobs in summer when the tourists come to stay in the hotels, and my parents decided that my mother should get such a job to earn extra money.

I said, "But what will we do? Won't we go to the mesa? What will Grandmother do?"

Mother said, "Kate, you are big, you will help Grandmother. Johnny will do his share. He is big enough to bring wood and water. Perhaps the neighbors will help with Grandmother's garden. But if the mesa springs are as dry as ours, perhaps there will not be much of a garden. When the summer is over and we come to get you, perhaps Grandmother will come with us and live here."

I did not think she would, but I did not say so.

So my father drove us to the mesa in the truck. It is about forty miles. We rode across the desert, between red and black and yellow rocks, and sand dunes covered with sage and yellow-flowered rabbit-brush. I was thinking about the work I would do. I don't mind the work, because it's important. Someday Grandmother's house will be Mother's, and then it will be mine. So I ought to know how to do everything.

11. Which one of the following events occurred first?
   a. Father took Kate and Johnny to Grandmother's house.
   b. Mother told Kate to help Grandmother.
   ⓒ Father and Mother decided that Mother should get a job in the summer.

12. In which place would you find colorful rocks?
   a. The mesa
   ⓑ The desert
   c. The sand dunes

13. Why did Kate think they should go to Grandmother's house?
   a. To see the sand dunes
   b. To make Johnny work
   ⓒ To help Grandmother

14. Which character encouraged Kate to help Grandmother?
   ⓐ Mother
   b. Father
   c. Johnny

15. What will Kate do when she arrives at Grandmother's house?
   ⓐ Help in the house and garden
   b. Watch television
   c. Make Johnny do all the work

16. How does Kate probably feel about helping Grandmother for the summer?
   a. She thinks she will be bored all summer.
   b. She feels sorry for herself.
   ⓒ She feels proud for being in charge of important work.

STOP - end of test - SCORE: _____

78   Reading Mastery Plus, Level 6

Recording Individual Results

(Use the following script to record individual results.)

1. Look at your Individual Skills Profile Chart.
2. You're going to record your test results for lesson 20. First look at the test to find out which items you got wrong. Then circle those items on the chart.
3. Now record your results. I'll help you if you have any questions. (Circulate among the students as they record their results.)
4. (After the students finish, say:) Now count the items you did *not* circle and write the total in the **Total** box near the bottom of the column. The total should be the same as your test score.
5. Now you'll fill in the other boxes for lesson 20. If you scored 0 to 12 points, write an **X** in the box marked **Retest.** If you scored 13 to 16 points, write your score in the box marked **FINAL SCORE.**

Remedial Exercises

Students who scored 0 to 12 points on the test should be given remedial help. After the regular reading period is over, assemble these students and present the following exercises. The students will need their original test papers.

EXERCISE 1   Vocabulary Review

1. Let's talk about the meanings of some words
2. The first word is **vow.** When you **vow** to do something, you promise to do it.
   - Everybody, what's another way of saying **I promise to be on time today**? (Signal.) *I vow to be on time today.*
3. The next word is **affair.** Something that is your **affair** is your business.
   - Everybody, what's another way of saying **That's not your business**? (Signal.) *That's not your affair.*

4. The next word is **smudge.** When you **smudge** something, you smear it.
   - Everybody, what's another way of saying **They accidentally smeared the wet paint**? (Signal.) *They accidentally smudged the wet paint.*
5. The next word is **neglect.** When you **neglect** something, you fail to take care of it.
   - Everybody, what's another way of saying **The boy failed to take care of the plants**? (Signal.) *The boy neglected the plants.*
6. The next word is **feeble.** Something that is very weak is **feeble.**
   - Everybody, what's another way of saying **He made a very weak attempt to kick the ball**? (Signal.) *He made a feeble attempt to kick the ball.*
7. The next word is **bewildered.** Someone who is **bewildered** is confused.
   - Everybody, what's another way of saying **The children were confused**? (Signal.) *The children were bewildered.*
8. The next word is **custom.** A way of behaving that everybody follows is a **custom.**
   - Everybody, what's another way of saying **When you travel, you learn about other ways of behaving**? (Signal.) *When you travel, you learn about other customs.*
9. The next word is **burro.** A small donkey is a **burro.**
   - Everybody, what's another way of saying **The farmer loaded the small donkey**? (Signal.) *The farmer loaded the burro.*
10. The last word is **gourd.** A **gourd** is a fruit with a hard shell.
    - Everybody, what's another way of saying **A fruit with a hard shell can be used as a tool**? (Signal.) *A gourd can be used as a tool.*

EXERCISE 2   General Review

1. How is a mesa like a table? (Idea: *It's flat on top.*)

2. Everybody, look at the passage on page 77 of your test. We're going to figure out the main idea of the paragraph.
(Call on a student to read the paragraph aloud. Correct any decoding errors.)

3. Who is the main character in the paragraph? (Response: *Grandmother.*)

4. What is the main thing that character is doing? (Idea: *Shaping a bowl.*)

5. So what is the main idea of the paragraph? (Idea: *Grandmother is shaping a bowl.*)

6. Name some supporting details for that main idea. (Ideas: *Grandmother used a gourd shell to shape the basket; she pushed from inside the basket until it was shaped like the curve of the gourd.*)

EXERCISE 3   Passage Reading

1. Everybody, look at the passage on page 78 of your test. You're going to read the passage aloud.

2. (Call on individual students to read several sentences each. Correct any decoding errors. When the students finish, present the following questions.)

3. Why did Mother need to stay in town for the summer? (Idea: *To earn extra money.*)

4. Who was concerned about Grandmother? (Response: *Kate.*)

5. Who will help Grandmother? (Ideas: *Kate; Johnny; Grandmother's neighbors.*)

6. What might Grandmother do at the end of the summer? (Idea: *Go to live with Kate's family.*)

7. Did Kate think Grandmother would do that? (Response: *No.*)

8. What did Kate see on the drive to Grandmother's? (Ideas: *The desert; sand dunes.*)

9. Why did Kate think the work at Grandmother's house was important? (Idea: *Someday the house would be hers, and she ought to know how to do everything.*)

Retesting the Students

After you've completed the remedial exercises, retest each student individually. To administer the retest, you will need the student's original test paper, a blank copy of the test, and a red pencil. Give the student the blank copy of the test. Say, "Look at page 77. You're going to take this test again. Read each item aloud and tell me the answer."

Use the student's original test paper to grade the retest. Use the red pencil to mark each correct answer with a **C** and each incorrect answer with an **X**. Then count one point for each correct answer and write the new score at the bottom of the page. Finally, revise the Individual Skills Profile Chart by drawing an **X** over any items the student missed on the retest.

Complete the Group Point Chart for lesson 20.

Administering the Checkouts

You can conduct checkouts by using the passage on page 78 of the Lesson 20 Mastery Test. A checkout takes about a minute and a half per student. See page 9 for a complete description of checkout procedures.

Tested Skills and Concepts

The Lesson 20 Mastery Test measures student mastery of the following skills and concepts.

- using vocabulary words in context (items 1–3)
- using context to predict word meaning (items 4–6)
- identifying literal cause and effect (item 7)
- making comparisons (item 8)
- inferring the main idea (item 9)
- inferring details relevant to a main idea (item 10)
- sequencing narrative events (item 11)
- distinguishing settings by features (item 12)
- interpreting a character's motives (item 13)
- distinguishing characters by trait (item 14)
- predicting a character's actions (item 15)
- interpreting a character's feelings (item 16)

Lesson 30

Administering the Test

The Lesson 30 Mastery Test should be administered after the students complete all work on lesson 30 and before they begin work on lesson 31. Each student will need a pencil and a copy of the test. Use the following script.

1. (Have the students clear their desks. Make sure each student has a pencil.)
2. Now you're going to take another test on what you've learned. This test will be longer than the others you've taken because it has questions about the last thirty lessons. I'll give each of you a copy of the test. Don't begin until I tell you. (Pass out the tests.)
3. Write your name on the name line in the upper right-hand corner of each page.
4. Now you're ready to begin the test. Answer all the items on each page. There is no time limit. When you've finished, turn your test facedown and look up at me. Begin the test now. (If you are including the writing item as part of the testing session, tell students they can begin the writing item after they finish the mastery test.)

Grading the Test

You can grade the tests yourself, or you can have the students grade one another's tests. If you want the students to grade one another's tests, tell them to trade test papers. Then use the following procedure.

1. Now we're going to grade the test. I'll read the correct answer for each item. If the answer is correct, mark it with a **C.** If the answer is wrong, mark it with an **X.**
2. (Read the correct answers from the answer key on this page and the next.)
3. Now count the number of **correct** answers and enter the score at the end of the test.

Answer Key

Lesson 30

Name _____

For items 1–12, circle the letter of the answer that means the same thing as the underlined part.

1. The manager was busy when I called, so the telephone operator told me to wait a minute.

   a. create a market
   b. sow the seeds of doom
   ⓒ hold the wire

2. Her winter jacket was lined with the fur of a sheep.

   a. batter
   b. tar
   ⓒ fleece

3. The entertainer tells stories and sings songs.

   a. suitor
   b. boar
   ⓒ minstrel

4. The farmer tilled the garden with a tool used to break up dirt.

   ⓐ hoe
   b. lasso
   c. squash

5. The painful illness made Dad a miserable person.

   a. goblin
   ⓑ wretch
   c. mirage

6. The spoiled child showed disrespect to the babysitter.

   ⓐ contempt
   b. one chance in ten
   c. palette

7. Liz took a risk when she tried out for the team.

   a. her turn
   b. a break
   ⓒ a chance

8. The festival was held in the plaza.

   ⓐ open area surrounded by walls or buildings
   b. apple or peach orchard
   c. petting area of a zoo

9. The army took revenge on the winner of the battle.

   a. sent a gift to
   ⓑ got even with
   c. was proud of

10. Did you tether the dog with the chain as I asked?

    ⓐ tie
    b. play with
    c. feed

11. The historic lunatic asylum is on the city tour.

    a. pool where manatees swim
    b. home where runaway slaves hid
    ⓒ place where insane people are kept

12. The hunter is stalking quail in the desert.

    ⓐ quietly following
    b. taking photographs of
    c. doing tricks with

Lesson 30 Test   79

Name _____

For items 13–48, circle the letter of the correct answer.

Lessons 1–10

13. During the 1930s, why did unemployed people go from town to town?

    a. To write about their travels
    ⓑ To look for work
    c. To visit other unemployed people

14. What did Aunt Agnes think Uncle Ulysses did with his spare time?

    ⓐ Frittered it away
    b. Napped
    c. Ate doughnuts

15. What is the most likely reason Mr. Gabby came into the lunch room?

    a. He smelled the doughnuts.
    b. He knew Uncle Ulysses.
    ⓒ He had nowhere else to go.

16. How did Homer solve the problem of the missing bracelet?

    a. By cutting all the doughnuts in half
    ⓑ By advertising a reward for the bracelet
    c. By giving Mr. Gabby a job

Read the passage below. Then answer items 17–21.

As the years went by, most of the people of Ithaca came to believe that Odysseus must be dead. Only his wife, Penelope, his son, Telemachus, and a few of his servants thought he was still alive.

With Odysseus gone, the people of Ithaca no longer had a king. Telemachus was too young to become the king, and Penelope was not allowed to take her husband's place. But any man who married Penelope could become the new king.

Many men wanted to marry Penelope, but she refused them all. After a while, these men decided to join together and stay at Odysseus's palace until Penelope agreed to marry one of them. They were called suitors, and there were more than a hundred of them. They did nothing but eat all day long, and nobody could stop them. They would never go away, they said, until Penelope chose one of them to be her husband and king of the island.

Year after year, Penelope kept hoping that Odysseus was still alive and would return soon. Telemachus hoped so, too, although he worried about what the suitors might do if Odysseus did return. They might kill Odysseus, and then Penelope would be forced to marry one of them.

17. Why did most of the people of Ithaca think Odysseus must be dead?

    ⓐ Because he had been gone for years
    b. Because Penelope believed he was dead
    c. Because his son said he saw him die

18. Which event happened last?

    a. Odysseus disappeared from Ithaca.
    ⓑ Penelope's suitors decided to stay at the palace.
    c. Many men asked Penelope to marry them.

19. What is the main idea of the passage?

    a. The suitors ate all day long at the palace.
    b. Penelope was not allowed to take her husband's place as ruler.
    ⓒ Because Odysseus was gone, many men wanted to marry Penelope.

20. What is one supporting detail for that main idea?

    a. Only Penelope, Telemachus, and a few servants thought Odysseus was still alive.
    ⓑ There were more than a hundred suitors.
    c. The suitors might kill Odysseus if he returned.

21. Which character was worried about what the suitors might do if Odysseus returned?

    ⓐ Telemachus
    b. Penelope
    c. Odysseus

80   Reading Mastery Plus, Level 6

14   Reading Mastery Plus, Level 6, Testing and Management Handbook

Lessons 11–20

22. According to Athena what did the eagle's attack show?

ⓐ Odysseus will take revenge on the suitors.
b. Odysseus will kill all the geese in the kingdom.
c. Odysseus is as strong as an eagle.

23. How was Odysseus disguised?

a. As an eagle
ⓑ As a beggar
c. As Athena

24. Why did Argos make one last effort to stand before he died?

a. The suitors ordered him to get up.
ⓑ He knew his master Odysseus.
c. He wanted to show how he used to hunt.

25. How did the nurse know that the beggar was Odysseus?

ⓐ She recognized the long scar on his leg.
b. He told her.
c. Telemachus told her.

Read the passage below. Then answer items 26–31.

The suitors warmed and greased the bow, and one after another they tried to bend it. Meanwhile, Eumayus and the cow farmer went out into the court, and Odysseus followed them. He asked them, "Whose side would you two take if Odysseus came home? Would you fight for him or for the suitors?"

"For Odysseus!" they both cried. "If only he would come!"

"He has come, and I am he!" said their master. Odysseus promised to give the two men land of their own if he was victorious, and he showed them the scar on his leg to prove who he was. The farmers hugged him and shed tears of joy. Then Odysseus told them to follow him back into the hall, where he would ask for the bow. He told Eumayus to place the bow in his hands no matter what the suitors said.

When the three men returned to the hall, Antinous was trying in vain to bend the bow. Finally, he begged to put off the test until the next day. On hearing that, Odysseus asked for a chance to string the bow. The suitors told him he could not, and they threatened him.

But Penelope said the beggar could try his strength. She agreed that he was not a suitor and she could not marry him if he succeeded. But she would give him new clothes, a sword, and a spear and would send him wherever he wanted to go.

26. Why did the suitors warm and grease the bow?

a. They were making it easier for Odysseus to string.
b. Whoever greased it best got to marry Penelope.
ⓒ Greasing the bow would make it easier to bend.

27. With whom did Eumayus and the cow farmer say they would side?

a. The suitors
ⓑ Odysseus
c. Antinous

28. Which event happened last?

ⓐ Penelope said the beggar could try his strength.
b. The suitors warmed and greased the bow.
c. Odysseus asked for a chance to string the bow.

29. Why did Odysseus want Eumayus to give him the bow?

a. He was going to kill the suitors with it.
b. He wanted to help Antinous.
ⓒ He knew he could string it.

30. Why did Penelope say she would give the beggar clothes, a sword, and a spear if he could string the bow?

a. He had only his beggar's clothing.
ⓑ He wasn't a suitor and thus couldn't marry her.
c. Clothes, a sword, and a spear were prizes for stringing the bow.

Read the passage below. Then answer items 43–48.

The third son apprenticed himself to a turner. Because turning is a difficult trade, it took him a long time to learn it. One day, he received a letter from his brothers with all their bad news. They explained how the innkeeper had stolen their treasures on the last night of their travels.

Finally, the young turner had learned his trade and was ready to travel around the world. To reward the apprentice for his good conduct, the master gave him a sack and told him there was a stick inside it.

"The sack may be useful to me," said the new journeyman. "But what is the good of the stick?"

"I will tell you," answered the master. "If anyone does you any harm, just say 'Stick, out of the sack!' Then the stick will jump out upon them and beat them so soundly that they will not be able to move for a week. It will not stop until you say, 'Stick, into the sack!' "

The journeyman thanked the master, took up the sack, and started on his travels. When anyone attacked him, he would say, "Stick, out of the sack!" Then the stick would immediately jump out and deal a shower of blows on the attacker, quickly ending the affair.

One evening, the young turner reached the inn where his two brothers had been fooled. He laid his sack on the table and began to describe all the wonderful things he had seen in the world.

"Yes," he said loudly, "you may talk of self-covering tables, gold-spitting donkeys, and so forth. These are good things, but they are nothing in comparison with the treasure I carry with me in my sack!"

Then the innkeeper opened his ears.

"What in the world can it be?" he thought. "Very likely the sack is full of precious stones. I have a perfect right to it, for all good things come in threes."

43. Why did the third son stay at the inn where his brothers had stayed?

a. He had heard the food was good there.
ⓑ He wanted to teach the innkeeper a lesson.
c. The stick told him to stay there.

44. What will the innkeeper probably do?

a. Attack the third son
b. Write a letter apologizing to the other two brothers
ⓒ Steal the sack

45. What did the innkeeper mean when he said all good things come in threes?

ⓐ Because he had the treasures of the other two brothers, he thought he should have the third son's treasure as well.
b. It was the third day of the month.
c. He also had three sons.

46. What will probably happen if the innkeeper tries to steal the sack?

a. The sack will turn to gold.
ⓑ The young turner will say, "Stick, out of the sack," and the stick will beat the innkeeper.
c. The young turner will write a letter to his brothers about the theft.

47. What will the young turner do after that?

a. Return to his master for another sack
ⓑ Find his brothers' treasures and go home
c. Warn other travelers about the dishonest innkeeper

48. Why did the innkeeper think the sack probably held precious stones?

a. Because the third son was a rich turner
b. Because the sack was very heavy
ⓒ Because the other two brothers had valuable treasures

STOP - end of test - SCORE: _____

---

31. How did Eumayus feel toward Odysseus?

ⓐ Loyal
b. Jealous
c. Embarrassed

Lessons 21–30

32. Here's a fact: *The man had a bad sunburn.* Which one of the following items is relevant to the fact?

a. The man was wearing a red shirt
ⓑ The man had spent the day on the beach.
c. The man had been playing with matches.

33. Here's a fact: *The dog was panting loudly.* Which one of the following items is irrelevant to the fact?

a. The dog had been running.
b. It was very hot outside.
ⓒ The dog was a poodle.

Read the facts below. Then answer items 34 and 35.

Fact A: Lila is wearing an apron.
Fact B: Lila is doing her homework.

34. Which one of the following statements is relevant to fact A?

ⓐ She lives in Ames, Iowa.
ⓑ She is making cookies.
c. Her favorite subject is math.

35. Which one of the following statements is relevant to fact B?

ⓐ She is using a calculator.
b. She plans to be a chef.
c. She has brown hair and blue eyes.

36. What do you call a young person who learns a craft from an older person?

a. A minstrel
ⓑ An apprentice
c. A saddle maker

37. Why did the length of the apprenticeship depend on the craft?

a. Some of the masters just wanted the apprentices to run errands.
b. The apprentices liked living at their masters' homes.
ⓒ Some crafts were more difficult to learn.

38. How did Mr. Warfield know the Dunns were growing a garden?

a. Mrs. Callahan told him.
ⓑ Water from Mrs. Dunn's watering can splashed on his head.
c. He saw the garden in a dream.

39. Which character claims to be "a reasonable person"?

a. Mrs. Dunn
b. Mrs. Grotowski
ⓒ Mr. Warfield

40. Why did Mr. Warfield agree to let the Dunns keep the garden?

ⓐ Mrs. Dunn let Mr. Warfield think it was his idea.
b. Mrs. Dunn threatened Mr. Warfield.
c. Mr. Dunn begged Mr. Warfield.

41. What would you find in an artists' colony?

ⓐ Many artists
b. Ants
c. Pilgrims

42. In "The Last Leaf," what is meant by the statement "Pneumonia was not a well-mannered stranger"?

a. The doctor had never seen pneumonia.
b. A person can get pneumonia from falling leaves.
ⓒ It was a serious disease and came with no warning.

Recording Individual Results

(Use the following script to record individual results.)

1. Look at your Individual Skills Profile Chart.
2. You're going to record your test results for lesson 30. First look at the test to find out which items you got wrong. Then circle those items on the chart.
3. Now record your results. I'll help you if you have any questions. (Circulate among the students as they record their results.)
4. (After the students finish, say:) Now count the items you did *not* circle and write the total in the **Total** box near the bottom of the column. The total should be the same as your test score.
5. Now you'll fill in the other boxes for lesson 30. If you scored 0 to 38 points, write an **X** in the box marked **Retest**. If you scored 39 to 48 points, write your score in the box marked **FINAL SCORE**.

Remedial Exercises

Students who scored 0 to 38 points on the test should be given remedial help. After the regular reading period is over, assemble these students and present the following exercises. The students will need their original test papers.

EXERCISE 1   Vocabulary Review

1. Let's talk about the meanings of some words.

2. The first term is **create a market.** When you **create a market,** you create a demand.
   - Everybody, what's another way of saying **The store created a demand for skateboards**? (Signal.) *The store created a market for skateboards.*

3. The next term is **sow the seeds of doom.** When you **sow the seeds of doom,** you plan how to punish someone.
   - Everybody, what's another way of saying **The king wanted the soldiers to plan how to punish the thief**? (Signal.) *The king wanted the soldiers to sow the seeds of doom for the thief.*

4. The next term is **hold the wire. Hold the wire** is another way of saying "wait a minute" when you're speaking on the telephone.
   - Everybody, if you're speaking on the telephone, what's another way of saying **Would you please wait a minute?** (Signal.) *Would you please hold the wire?*

5. The next word is **batter.** Ingredients for doughnuts and pancakes are **batter.**
   - Everybody, what's another way of saying **Pour the pancake ingredients into the pan now**? (Signal.) *Pour the pancake batter into the pan now.*

6. The next word is **tar. Tar** is a hard, black substance that turns into a sticky mass when heated.
   - Everybody, what's another way of saying **The road had been covered with a hard, black substance**? (Signal.) *The road had been covered with tar.*

7. The next word is **fleece.** The fur of a sheep is called **fleece.**
   - Everybody, what's another way of saying **Her jacket is lined with the fur of a sheep**? (Signal.) *Her jacket is lined with fleece.*

8. The next word is **suitor.** A man who wants to marry a woman is that woman's **suitor.**
   - Everybody, what's another way of saying **The man who wants to marry Jean bought her a ring**? (Signal.) *Jean's suitor bought her a ring.*

9. The next word is **boar.** A **boar** is a wild pig.
   - Everybody, what's another way of saying **We saw a wild pig at the zoo**? (Signal.) *We saw a boar at the zoo.*

10. The next word is **minstrel.** A **minstrel** is an entertainer who tells stories and sings songs.
    - Everybody, what's another way of saying **My great-grandfather was an entertainer who told stories and sang songs**? (Signal.) *My great-grandfather was a minstrel.*

11. The next word is **hoe.** A **hoe** is a tool used to break up dirt.
    - Everybody, what tool would you use to break up dirt? (Signal.) *A hoe.*

12. The next word is **lasso.** A **lasso** is a rope used to catch horses and cattle.
    - Everybody, what kind of a rope does a cowhand use to to catch horses and cattle? (Signal.) *A lasso.*

13. The next word is **squash.** A **squash** is a vegetable that is like a pumpkin.
    - Everybody, what's another of saying **We baked a vegetable that is like a pumpkin**? (Signal.) *We baked a squash.*

14. The next word is **goblin.** A **goblin** is an ugly and wicked fairy.
    - Everybody, what's another way of saying **I had a nightmare about an ugly and wicked fairy**? (Signal.) *I had a nightmare about a goblin.*

15. The next word is **wretch.** Someone who is a miserable person is a **wretch.**
    - Everybody, what's another way of saying **When she is sick, she is a miserable person**? (Signal.) *When she is sick, she is a wretch.*

16. The next word is **mirage.** Something that seems to be there but is really not there is a **mirage.**
    - Everybody, what's another way of saying **The thirsty hikers saw a pool of water that was not really there**? (Signal.) *The thirsty hikers saw a mirage.*

17. The next word is **contempt. Contempt** is another word for **disrespect.**
    - Everybody, what's another way of saying **Disrespect toward the camp counselors is against the rules**? (Signal.) *Contempt toward the camp counselors is against the rules.*

18. The next term is **one chance in ten.** If there is **one chance in ten** that somebody in a group of ten people will win a prize, one of those people will probably win a prize.
    - Everybody, what are the chances that one of the people in a group of ten will win a prize? (Signal.) *One chance in ten.*

19. The next word is **palette.** A **palette** is a thin board that artists use for mixing paint.
    - Everybody, what's another way of saying **The artist mixed the paint on a thin board**? (Signal.) *The artist mixed the paint on a palette.*

20. The next word is **risk.** When you take a **risk,** you take a chance.
    - Everybody, what's another way of saying **If you drive faster than the speed limit, you are taking a big chance**? (Signal.) *If you drive faster than the speed limit, you are taking a big risk.*

21. The next word is **plaza.** When you are in a plaza, you are in an open area surrounded by walls or buildings.
    - Everybody, what's another way of saying **We'll meet you in the open area surrounded by walls**? (Signal.) *We'll meet you in the plaza.*

22. The next word is **revenge.** When people take **revenge,** they get even.
    - Everybody, what do you do if you take revenge on someone? (Signal.) *You get even.*

23. The next word is **tether. Tether** means "to tie with a rope or a chain to an object."
    - Everybody, what's another way of saying **Sheila always ties her horse with a rope to the fence post**? (Signal.) *Sheila always tethers her horse.*

24. The last word is **stalk.** When a hunter **stalks** an animal, the hunter follows it quietly.
    - Everybody, what's another way of saying **The cougar is quietly following the wounded deer**? (Signal.) *The cougar is stalking the wounded deer.*

EXERCISE 2   General Review

1. What do we call information that helps explain a fact? (Response: *Relevant information.*)
   - What do we call information that does not help explain a fact? (Response: *Irrelevant information.*)

2. Here's a fact. **A man was shivering.**
   - Here's some information: **The man was named Fred.** Is that information **relevant** or **irrelevant** to the fact? (Response: *Irrelevant.*)
   - Here's some more information: **The man was standing in the cold.** Is that information **relevant** or **irrelevant** to the fact? (Response: *Relevant.*)

3. What kind of business did Uncle Ulysses and Aunt Agnes have? (Idea: *A lunchroom.*)

4. What is a sandwich sign? (Idea: *A sign with one part that hangs in front of a person and one part that hangs behind.*)

5. What was printed on the sandwich signs? (Idea: *Advertisements.*)

6. What did the lady help Homer do? (Idea: *Make doughnuts.*)

7. What did she lose in the doughnut batter? (Idea: *Her diamond bracelet.*)

8. How was Athena disguised when she visited Telemachus? (Idea: *As a servant.*)

9. What did the eagle swoop down and carry off? (Idea: *A large white goose.*)

10. What did Athena say this meant? (Idea: *That Odysseus would return home and take revenge on the suitors.*)

11. Who was the master of Argos? (Idea: *Odysseus.*)

12. What was Argos known as? (Idea: *The keenest hunter of them all.*)

13. What do you call a child who works without pay to learn a craft? (Response: *An apprentice.*)

14. How young were some of these children? (Idea: *As young as ten.*)

15. What kinds of crafts did they learn? (Ideas: *Making shoes; weaving cloth; making furniture; making saddles.*)

16. What do you call the person for whom an apprentice worked? (Response: *A master.*)

17. How long might it take to learn to be a baker? (Response: *Two or three years.*)

18. How long might it take to learn to be a saddle maker? (Response: *Up to ten years.*)

19. What would an apprentice become after he or she learned the craft? (Response: *A journeyman.*)

20. Who was growing a garden? (Idea: *The Dunn family.*)

21. What were they raising and growing? (Ideas: *Hens; vegetables; spices.*)

22. What kind of man did Mr. Warfield call himself? (Idea: *A reasonable man.*)

23. Here's a main idea from "The Last Leaf": **Joan thought she was going to die.**
    - Name some supporting details for that main idea. (Ideas: *Joan had pneumonia; Joan was watching the leaves fall; Joan thought she was like a falling leaf.*)

EXERCISE 3   Passage Reading

Passage 1

1. Everybody, look at the passage on page 80 of your test. You're going to read the passage aloud.

2. (Call on individual students to read several sentences each. Correct any decoding errors. When the students finish, present the following questions.)

3. At the beginning of the passage, how long had Odysseus been gone? (Idea: *Years.*)

4. Why couldn't Telemachus be king? (Idea: *He was too young.*)

5. Who could become king? (Idea: *Any man who married Penelope.*)

6. What were the men called who wanted to marry Penelope? (Idea: *Suitors.*)

7. How many suitors were there? (Idea: *More than a hundred.*)

8. What did Telemachus fear would happen if Odysseus returned? (Idea: *The suitors might kill Odysseus, and then Penelope would be forced to marry one of them.*)

Passage 2

1. Everybody, look at the passage on page 81 of your test. You're going to read the passage aloud.

2. (Call on individual students to read several sentences each. Correct any decoding errors. When the students finish, present the following questions.)

3. What did the suitors do to the bow? (Ideas: *Warmed and greased it; tried to bend it.*)

4. What did Odysseus ask Eumayus and the cow farmer? (Idea: *Whose side they would take if Odysseus came home.*)

5. What did Odysseus promise the two men if he were victorious? (Idea: *Land of their own.*)

6. What did he show them to prove who he was? (Idea: *The scar on his leg.*)

7. What did Odysseus ask for a chance to do? (Response: *String the bow.*)

8. What was the suitors' response to his request? (Ideas: *They told him he couldn't; they threatened him.*)

Passage 3

1. Everybody, look at the passage on page 83 of your test. You're going to read the passage aloud.

2. (Call on individual students to read several sentences each. Correct any decoding errors. When the students finish, present the following questions.)

3. What craft did the third son learn? (Response: *Turning.*)

4. How did he learn about his brothers' bad news? (Idea: *They wrote him a letter.*)

5. Why did the master reward the young turner? (Idea: *Because of his good conduct.*)

6. What did the master give the young turner? (Idea: *A sack and a stick.*)

7. What did the master tell the young turner to say if anyone tried to harm him? (Response: *Stick, out of the sack!*)

8. To what did the young turner compare his sack? (Idea: *Self-covering tables and gold-spitting donkeys.*)

9. What did the innkeeper think was probably in the sack? (Response: *Precious stones.*)

Retesting the Students

After you've completed the remedial exercises, retest each student individually. To administer the retest, you will need the student's original test paper, a blank copy of the test, and a red pencil. Give the student the blank copy of the test. Say, "Look at page 79. You're going to take this test again. Read each item aloud and tell me the answer."

Use the student's original test paper to grade the retest. Use the red pencil to mark each correct answer with a **C** and each incorrect answer with an **X**. Then count one point for each correct answer and write the new score at the bottom of the page. Finally, revise the Individual Skills Profile Chart by drawing an **X** over any items the student missed on the retest.

Complete the Group Point Chart for lesson 30.

Administering the Checkouts

You can conduct checkouts by using the passage on page 83 of the Lesson 30 Mastery Test. See page 9 for a complete description of checkout procedures.

Tested Skills and Concepts

The Lesson 30 Mastery Test measures student mastery of the following skills and concepts.

- using vocabulary words in context (items 1–6)
- using context to predict word meaning (items 7–12)
- identifying literal cause and effect (items 13 and 25)
- interpreting a character's feelings (items 14 and 17)
- interpreting a character's motives (items 15 and 29)
- evaluating problems and solutions (items 16 and 30)
- sequencing narrative events (items 18 and 28)
- inferring the main idea (item 19)
- inferring details relevant to a main idea (item 20)
- distinguishing characters by trait (items 21 and 39)
- making comparisons (item 22)
- recalling details and events (items 23 and 38)
- inferring story details and events (items 24 and 48)
- inferring causes and effects (items 26 and 43)
- answering literal questions about a text (items 27 and 36)
- drawing conclusions (items 31 and 37)
- identifying relevant evidence (items 32–35)
- inferring a character's point of view (item 40)
- distinguishing settings by features (item 41)
- interpreting figurative language (items 42 and 45)
- predicting narrative outcomes (items 44 and 46)
- predicting a character's actions (item 47)

Lesson 40

Administering the Test

The Lesson 40 Mastery Test should be administered after the students complete all work on lesson 40 and before they begin work on lesson 41. Each student will need a pencil and a copy of the test. Use the following script.

1. (Have the students clear their desks. Make sure each student has a pencil.)
2. Now you're going to take another test on what you've learned. I'll give each of you a copy of the test. Don't begin until I tell you. (Pass out the tests.)
3. Write your name on the name line in the upper right-hand corner of each page.
4. Now you're ready to begin the test. Answer all the items on each page. There is no time limit. When you've finished, turn your test facedown and look up at me. Begin the test now. (If you are including the writing item as part of the testing session, tell students they can begin the writing item after they finish the mastery test.)

Grading the Test

You can grade the tests yourself, or you can have the students grade one another's tests. If you want the students to grade one another's tests, tell them to trade test papers. Then use the following script.

1. Now we're going to grade the test. I'll read the correct answer for each item. If the answer is correct, mark it with a **C**. If the answer is wrong, mark it with an **X**.
2. (Read the correct answers from the answer key in the next column.)
3. Now count the number of **correct** answers and enter the score at the end of the test.

Answer Key

Lesson 40

Name _____

For items 1–6, circle the letter of the answer that means the same thing as the underlined part.

1. We felt sad and lonely when our favorite teacher retired.
   a. exquisite
   b. forlorn
   c. distinguished

2. The detective tried to find a reason for the crime.
   a. twitch
   b. plume
   c. motive

3. The girl threw away the broken cup.
   a. detained
   b. discarded
   c. summoned

4. The small but triumphant army marched proudly into the city.
   a. victorious
   b. defeated
   c. wretched

5. Did you behold the beautiful sunset?
   a. photograph
   b. observe
   c. draw

6. Mrs. Hagashi suddenly recollected where her keys were.
   a. gathered
   b. remembered
   c. remained

84   Reading Mastery Plus, Level 6

For items 7–17, circle the letter of the correct answer.

7. How is Demeter different from Hades?
   a. Demeter is Greek.
   b. Demeter helps plants grow.
   c. Demeter is related to Zeus.

8. Who was Demeter's daughter?
   a. Olympus
   b. Cerberus
   c. Persephone

9. Why couldn't the sea nymphs go onto dry land?
   a. They would dry up.
   b. They had no clothing.
   c. They didn't want to be eaten by wolves.

10. Where did Hades come from?
    a. Mount Olympus
    b. The bottomless hole
    c. The sea

11. Here's a main idea from the story of Persephone: *Demeter prevented the plants from growing.*
    What is one supporting detail for that main idea?
    a. Demeter carried a torch.
    b. The earth turned brown.
    c. Demeter met with Hecate.

Read the passage below. Then answer items 12–17.

Sara was a pupil at Miss Minchin's boarding school. One day, Sara found out that her father had died. Miss Minchin called Sara into the parlor and said, "Everything will be different now. I sent for you to talk to you and make you understand. Your father is dead. You have no friends. You have no money. You have no home and no one to take care of you."

Name _____

Sara's pale little face twitched nervously, but her green-gray eyes did not move from Miss Minchin's—and still Sara said nothing.

"What are you staring at?" demanded Miss Minchin sharply. "Are you so stupid that you don't understand what I mean? I tell you that you are quite alone in the world and have no one to do anything for you, unless I choose to keep you here."

Miss Minchin could not bear to find herself with a little beggar on her hands.

"Now listen to me," she went on, "and remember what I say, If you work hard and make yourself useful, I shall let you stay here. You are only a child, but you are a very sharp child, and you learn things almost without being taught. You speak French very well, and in a year or so, you can begin to help with the younger pupils. By the time you are fifteen, you ought to be able to do that much at least."

Miss Minchin was a clever business woman. She knew that this determined child could be very useful to her and save her the trouble of paying large salaries to French teachers.

12. Why was Miss Minchin so angry with Sara?
    a. Sara was rude to her.
    b. Sara did not have any money.
    c. Sara did not want to teach French.

13. What problem would Miss Minchin solve by having Sara teach French?
    a. She could help Sara improve her French.
    b. She would not have to pay a French teacher.
    c. She could help Sara earn money.

14. What would Miss Minchin probably do if Sara had a lot of money?
    a. Send Sara to another school
    b. Keep Sara as a pupil
    c. Help Sara earn more money

15. Why didn't any of Sara's relatives come to help her?
    a. Her relatives trusted Miss Minchin.
    b. Her relatives lived far away.
    c. She had no one to take care of her.

16. After Sara's father died, why did Miss Minchin decide to keep Sara at the school?
    a. Sara could teach Greek.
    b. Sara's father had given her money.
    c. Sara could be useful to her.

17. Which character was clever at business?
    a. Sara
    b. Sara's father
    c. Miss Minchin

STOP - end of test - SCORE: _____

Lesson 40 Test   85

Recording Individual Results

(Use the following script to record individual results.)

1. Look at your Individual Skills Profile Chart.
2. You're going to record your test results for lesson 40. First look at the test to find out which items you got wrong. Then circle those items on the chart.
3. Now record your results. I'll help you if you have any questions. (Circulate among the students as they record their results.)
4. (After the students finish, say:) Now count the items you did *not* circle and write the total in the **Total** box near the bottom of the column. The total should be the same as your test score.
5. Now you'll fill in the other boxes for lesson 40. If you scored 0 to 13 points, write an **X** in the box marked **Retest.** If you scored 14 to 17 points, write your score in the box marked **FINAL SCORE.**

Remedial Exercises

Students who scored 0 to 13 points on the test should be given remedial help. After the regular reading period is over, assemble these students and present the following exercises. The students will need their original test papers.

EXERCISE 1   Vocabulary Review

1. Let's talk about the meanings of some words.

2. The first word is **forlorn. Forlorn** means "sad and lonely."
   - Everybody, what's another way of saying **The man was sad and lonely**? (Signal.) *The man was forlorn.*

3. The next word is **motive.** A person's **motive** for doing something is the person's reason for doing that thing.
   - Everybody, what's another way of saying **The boy had a special reason for going to school early**? (Signal.) *The boy had a special motive for going to school early.*

4. The next word is **detained.** When you are **detained,** you are held against your will.
   - Everybody, what's another way of saying **The police held him against his will**? (Signal.) *The police detained him.*

5. The next word is **discard.** When you **discard** something, you throw it away.
   - Everybody, what's another way of saying **The woman threw away the empty bottle**? (Signal.) *The woman discarded the empty bottle.*

6. The next word is **summon.** When you **summon** someone, you order that person to go somewhere.
   - Everybody, what's another way of saying **The coach ordered the players to the locker room**? (Signal.) *The coach summoned the players to the locker room.*

7. The next word is **triumphant. Triumphant** is another word for **victorious.**
   - Everybody, what's another way of saying **The team was victorious**? (Signal.) *The team was triumphant.*

8. The next word is **behold. Behold** is another word for **observe.**
   - Everybody, what's another way of saying **Did you observe the mountains?** (Signal.) *Did you behold the mountains?*

9. The last word is **recollect.** When you **recollect** something, you remember it.
   - Everybody, what's another way of saying **The man could not remember his name**? (Signal.) *The man could not recollect his name.*

EXERCISE 2   General Review

1. Who was Demeter? (Idea: *The goddess of the earth.*)

2. What was Olympus? (Idea: *A mountain.*)
   - What was Cerberus? (Idea: *Hades' dog.*)
   - Who was Persephone? (Idea: *Demeter's daughter.*)

3. Why did the sea nymphs let the waves break over them every moment or two? (Idea: *To keep them moist*.)
   - What did they say they would look like if they didn't keep moist? (Idea: *A bunch of dried seaweed*.)

4. Who lived on Mount Olympus? (Idea: *Zeus*.)
   - Who lived in the bottomless hole? (Idea: *Hades*.)
   - Who lived in the sea? (Idea: *The sea nymphs*.)

EXERCISE 3   Passage Reading

1. Everybody, look at the passage on pages 84 and 85 of your test. You're going to read the passage aloud.

2. (Call on individual students to read several sentences each. Correct any decoding errors. When the students finish, present the following questions.)

3. How did Miss Minchin earn money? (Idea: *By charging students to go to her school*.)
   - Could Sara pay Miss Minchin any money now? (Response: *No*.)
   - So how did Miss Minchin feel toward Sara? (Idea: *Angry*.)
   - What might change Miss Minchin's feelings about Sara? (Idea: *If Sara got money*.)

4. What could Sara teach the younger pupils? (Response: *French*.)
   - Why did Miss Minchin like the idea of giving Sara the job of teaching French? (Idea: *Because she wouldn't have to pay a real French teacher*.)

5. Why did Sara have to stay with Miss Minchin? (Ideas: *She had nowhere else to go; she had no friends or home*.)

Retesting the Students

After you've completed the remedial exercises, retest each student individually. To administer the retest, you will need the student's original test paper, a blank copy of the test, and a red pencil. Give the student the blank copy of the test. Say, "Look at page 84. You're going to take this test again. Read each item aloud and tell me the answer."

Use the student's original test paper to grade the retest. Use the red pencil to mark each correct answer with a **C** and each incorrect answer with an **X**. Then count one point for each correct answer and write the new score at the bottom of the page. Finally, revise the Individual Skills Profile Chart by drawing an **X** over any items the student missed on the retest.

Complete the Group Point Chart for lesson 40.

Administering the Checkouts

You can conduct checkouts by using the passage on pages 84 and 85 of the Lesson 40 Mastery Test. See page 9 for a complete description of checkout procedures.

Tested Skills and Concepts

The Lesson 40 Mastery Test measures student mastery of the following skills and concepts.

- using vocabulary words in context (items 1–3)
- using context to predict word meaning (items 4–6)
- making comparisons (item 7)
- recalling details and events (item 8)
- identifying literal cause and effect (item 9)
- distinguishing settings by features (item 10)
- inferring details relevant to a main idea (item 11)
- interpreting a character's feelings (item 12)
- evaluating problems and solutions (item 13)
- predicting a character's actions (item 14)
- inferring story details and events (item 15)
- interpreting a character's motives (item 16)
- distinguishing characters by trait (item 17)

Lesson 50

Administering the Test

The Lesson 50 Mastery Test should be administered after the students complete all work on lesson 50 and before they begin work on lesson 51. Each student will need a pencil and a copy of the test. Use the following script.

1. (Have the students clear their desks. Make sure each student has a pencil.)
2. Now you're going to take another test on what you've learned. I'll give each of you a copy of the test. Don't begin until I tell you. (Pass out the tests.)
3. Write your name on the name line in the upper right-hand corner of each page.
4. Now you're ready to begin the test. Answer all the items on each page. There is no time limit. When you've finished, turn your test facedown and look up at me. Begin the test now. (If you are including the writing item as part of the testing session, tell students they can begin the writing item after they finish the mastery test.)

Grading the Test

You can grade the tests yourself, or you can have the students grade one another's tests. If you want the students to grade one another's tests, tell them to trade test papers. Then use the following script.

1. Now we're going to grade the test. I'll read the correct answer for each item. If the answer is correct, mark it with a **C.** If the answer is wrong, mark it with an **X.**
2. (Read the correct answers from the answer key in the next column.)
3. Now count the number of correct answers and enter the score at the end of the test.

Answer Key

Lesson 50   Name _____

For items 1–6, circle the letter of the answer that means the same thing as the underlined part.

1. The expensive hotel was <u>elegant</u> in every way.

   (a) luxurious
   b. bedraggled
   c. drab

2. The wise woman <u>thought about</u> the meaning of life.

   (a) pondered
   b. caressed
   c. jostled

3. The <u>very faithful</u> hound waited for its master.

   a. vague
   b. impudent
   (c) devoted

4. The man <u>shuffled</u> carrying the heavy load.

   a. skipped happily
   (b) walked slowly
   c. jumped high

5. Did you <u>vent your anger</u> when you got into the accident?

   a. hide your anger
   b. call the police
   (c) let your anger show

6. Mom received a <u>parcel</u> on her birthday.

   a. summons
   b. telegram
   (c) package

For items 7–17, circle the letter of the correct answer.

7. Here's a simile: *In summer, the city was like an oven.*
   What does that simile mean?

   a. The city was made of metal.
   b. The city had a door.
   (c) The city was very hot.

8. Here's an exaggeration: *The baseball player hit the ball a mile.*
   What did the baseball player really do?

   a. Hit the ball one mile away
   b. Hit the ball ten feet away
   (c) Hit the ball a long way

9. Here's a metaphor: *The dancer was a swan in flight.*
   To what is the dancer being compared?

   a. A plane
   (b) A bird
   c. A sled

10. Here's a statement. *The con man was a sly fox.*
    What type of figurative language does that statement use?

    a. Simile
    (b) Metaphor
    c. Exaggeration

11. Here's a statement. *I'm so tired I could sleep for a year.*
    What type of figurative language does that statement use?

    a. Simile
    b. Metaphor
    (c) Exaggeration

86   Reading Mastery Plus, Level 6

Name _____

Read the passage below. Then answer items 12–17.

A few nights later, a very odd thing happened. Sara found something in the room that she certainly would never have expected. When she came in as usual, she saw something small and dark in her chair—an odd, tiny figure, which turned a small and weird-looking face toward her.
"Why, it's the monkey!" Sara cried. "It is the Indian Gentleman's monkey!"
It was the monkey, sitting up and looking forlorn. Very soon, Sara found out how he had gotten into her room. The skylight was open, and it was easy to guess that he had crept out of his master's garret window, which was only a few feet away. The monkey had probably been attracted by the light in Sara's attic and had crept in. And there he was.
When Sara went up to the monkey, he actually put out his elfish little hands, caught her dress, and jumped into her arms.
"Oh, you poor little thing!" said Sara, caressing him. "I can't help liking you, but you have such a forlorn look on your little face."
The monkey sat and looked at Sara while she talked. He seemed much interested in her remarks, judging by his eyes and his forehead and the way he moved his head up and down. He examined her quite seriously. He felt the material of her dress, touched her hands, climbed up and examined her ears, and then sat on her shoulder holding a lock of her hair, looking mournful but not at all agitated. Upon the whole, the monkey seemed pleased with Sara.
"I must take you back," she said to the monkey, "though I'm sorry to have to do it. Oh, you would be good company!"

12. What is the main idea of the passage?

    a. The monkey's master had garret windows.
    (b) A friendly little monkey came into Sara's room.
    c. The monkey held a lock of Sara's hair.

13. What is one supporting detail for that main idea?

    (a) The monkey jumped into Sara's arms.
    b. Sara lived in London.
    c. Sara was a student of Miss Minchin's.

14. What is the most likely reason the monkey looked forlorn?

    (a) He wanted to go back to his master.
    b. Sara said his face was weird looking.
    c. He didn't like the light in the attic.

15. How did the monkey examine Sara?

    a. Roughly
    b. Lightly
    (c) Seriously

16. What is the last thing Sara did?

    a. Went up to the monkey
    b. Saw something in her chair
    (c) Talked to the monkey

17. Why did Sara keep talking to the monkey?

    a. He looked mournful.
    b. She wanted to talk him into staying with her.
    (c) He seemed to understand what she was saying.

STOP - end of test - SCORE: _____

Lesson 50 Test   87

Recording Individual Results

(Use the following script to record individual results.)

1. Look at your Individual Skills Profile Chart.
2. You're going to record your test results for lesson 50. First look at the test to find out which items you got wrong. Then circle those items on the chart.
3. Now record your results. I'll help you if you have any questions. **(Circulate among the students as they record their results.)**
4. (After the students finish, say:) Now count the items you did *not* circle and write the total in the **Total** box near the bottom of the column. The total should be the same as your test score.
5. Now you'll fill in the other boxes for lesson 50. If you scored 0 to 13 points, write an **X** in the box marked **Retest.** If you scored 14 to 17 points, write your score in the box marked **FINAL SCORE.**

Remedial Exercises

Students who scored 0 to 13 points on the test should be given remedial help. After the regular reading period is over, assemble these students and present the following exercises. The students will need their original test papers.

EXERCISE 1   Vocabulary Review

1. Let's talk about the meanings of some words.

2. The first word is **luxurious. Luxurious** is another word for **elegant.**
   • Everybody, what's another way of saying **She likes elegant fabrics**? (Signal.) *She likes luxurious fabrics.*

3. The next word is **bedraggled. Bedraggled** means "muddy and limp."
   • Everybody, what's another way of saying **The dog's hair was muddy and limp**? (Signal.) *The dog's hair was bedraggled.*

4. The next word is **drab. Drab** is another word for **dreary.**
   • Everybody, what's another way of saying **It is a cloudy, dreary day**? (Signal.) *It is a cloudy, drab day.*

5. The next word is **ponder.** When you think about something, you **ponder** it.
   • Everybody, what's another way of saying **The girl thought about her future**? (Signal.) *The girl pondered her future.*

6. The next word is **caress. Caress** means "lightly stroke."
   • Everybody, what's another way of saying **The cat likes to be lightly stroked**? (Signal.) *The cat likes to be caressed.*

7. The next word is **jostled.** When you are pushed and jolted, you are **jostled.**
   • Everybody, what's another way of saying **The girl was pushed and jolted by the crowd**? (Signal.) *The girl was jostled by the crowd.*

8. The next word is **vague. Vague** is another word for **unclear.**
   • Everybody, what's another way of saying **The directions to the picnic were unclear**? (Signal.) *The directions to the picnic were vague.*

9. The last word is **impudent.** Someone who is **impudent** is rude and bold.
   • Everybody, what's another way of saying **The teacher scolded the rude and bold girl**? (Signal.) *The teacher scolded the impudent girl.*

10. The next word is **devoted.** Someone who is **devoted** is very loyal.
    • Everybody, what's another way of saying **The very loyal dog stayed with its master**? (Signal.) *The devoted dog stayed with its master.*

11. The next word is **shuffle. Shuffle** means "to walk slowly and drag one's feet."
    • Everybody, what's another way of saying **Don't walk slowly and drag your feet**? (Signal.) *Don't shuffle.*

12. The next word is **vent.** When you vent your emotions, you let them show.
    - Everybody, what's another way of saying **When I am mad, I let my anger show**? (Signal.) *When I am mad, I vent my anger.*

13. The last word is **parcel. Parcel** is another word for **package.**
    - Everybody, what's another way of saying **I received a package in the mail**? (Signal.) *I received a parcel in the mail.*

EXERCISE 2   General Review

1. Here's a simile: **His skin was like sandpaper.**
    - How could his skin and sandpaper be the same? (Idea: *Both could be rough and scratchy.*)
    - So what does the simile mean? (Idea: *His skin was rough and scratchy.*)

2. Here's an exaggeration: **Her voice was deafening.**
    - Could a voice really make you deaf? (Response: *No.*)
    - What was her voice really like? (Idea: *Very loud.*)

3. Here's a metaphor: **The police officer barked commands to the drivers.**
    - To what is the police officer's voice being compared? (Idea: *A barking dog's.*)
    - So what does the metaphor mean? (Idea: *The police officer had a loud, rough voice.*)

4. What kind of figurative language compares things by using the word **like**? (Response: *A simile.*)
    - What kind of figurative language compares things without using the word **like**? (Response: *A metaphor.*)
    - What kind of figurative language stretches the truth? (Response: *Exaggeration.*)

EXERCISE 3   Passage Reading

1. Everybody, look at the passage on page 87 of your test. You're going to read the passage aloud.

2. (Call on individual students to read several sentences each. Correct any decoding errors. When the students finish, present the following questions.)

3. I'll read a paragraph from the passage: *When Sara went up to the monkey, he actually put out his elfish little hands, caught her dress, and jumped into her arms.*
    - The paragraph mentions several things the monkey did. What were those things? (Ideas: *He put out his hands; he caught Sara's dress; he jumped into her arms.*)
    - So what's the main idea of the paragraph? (Idea: *The monkey was playful and friendly.*)

4. In what ways did the monkey show his interest in Sara? (Ideas: *He moved his head up and down; he felt her dress, her hands, her ears, and her hair.*)

5. What does the monkey look like? (Idea: *He is small and dark and has a weird-looking face.*)

6. How does the monkey act? (Ideas: *Forlorn; mournful; interested in Sara's remarks.*)

7. Why does Sara want the monkey to stay? (Ideas: *He seems to like her; he would be good company.*)

Retesting the Students

After you've completed the remedial exercises, retest each student individually. To administer the retest, you will need the student's original test paper, a blank copy of the test, and a red pencil. Give the student the blank copy of the test. Say, "Look at page 86. You're going to take this test again. Read each item aloud and tell me the answer."

Use the student's original test paper to grade the retest. Use the red pencil to mark each correct answer with a **C** and each incorrect answer with an **X.** Then count one point for each correct answer and write the new score at the bottom of the page. Finally, revise the Individual Skills Profile Chart by drawing an **X** over any items the student missed on the retest.

Complete the Group Point Chart for lesson 50.

Administering the Checkouts

You can conduct checkouts by using the passage on page 87 of the Lesson 50 Mastery Test. See page 9 for a complete description of checkout procedures.

Tested Skills and Concepts

The Lesson 50 Mastery Test measures student mastery of the following skills and concepts.

- using vocabulary words in context (items 1–3)
- using context to predict word meaning (items 4–6)
- interpreting figurative language (items 7–11)
- inferring the main idea (item 12)
- inferring details relevant to a main idea (item 13)
- inferring a character's point of view (item 14)
- answering literal questions about a text (item 15)
- sequencing narrative events (item 16)
- drawing conclusions (item 17)

Lesson 60

Administering the Test

The Lesson 60 Mastery Test should be administered after the students complete all work on lesson 60 and before they begin work on lesson 61. Each student will need a pencil and a copy of the test. Use the following script.

1. (Have the students clear their desks. Make sure each student has a pencil.)
2. Now you're going to take another test on what you've learned. This test will be longer than the others you've taken because it has questions about the last thirty lessons. I'll give each of you a copy of the test. Don't begin until I tell you. (Pass out the tests.)
3. Write your name on the name line in the upper right-hand corner of each page.
4. Now you're ready to begin the test. Answer all the items on each page. There is no time limit. When you've finished, turn your test facedown and look up at me. Begin the test now. (If you are including the writing item as part of the testing session, tell students they can begin the writing item after they finish the mastery test.)

Grading the Test

You can grade the tests yourself, or you can have the students grade one another's tests. If you want the students to grade one another's tests, tell them to trade test papers. Then use the following script.

1. Now we're going to grade the test. I'll read the correct answer for each item. If the answer is correct, mark it with a **C.** If the answer is wrong, mark it with an **X.**
2. (Read the correct answers from the answer key on this page and the next.)
3. Now count the number of **correct** answers and enter the score at the end of the test.

Answer Key

Lesson 60

Name _____

For items 1–12, circle the letter of the answer that means the same thing as the underlined part.

1. My grandmother was weak and delicate for a few weeks after her illness.
   a. decked out
   b. obliged
   c. frail ✓

2. Our group came up with a great plan for our project.
   a. proposal ✓
   b. incident
   c. miscalculation

3. It was difficult for Karl to tolerate the long and boring speech.
   a. endure ✓
   b. maneuver
   c. spurn

4. We had a nice dinner at the party after the wedding.
   a. reception ✓
   b. parasol
   c. hostler

5. Did someone tell the ending of the mystery?
   a. efface
   b. reveal ✓
   c. croon

6. Mom's old and hard-to-find silver pattern might be in antique stores.
   a. rare ✓
   b. humiliating
   c. gallant

7. The tragic movie was full of melancholy characters.
   a. violent
   b. sarcastic
   c. sad ✓

8. That absurd ending just cannot be true.
   a. ridiculous ✓
   b. nonfiction
   c. serious

9. The bird sat on the largest bough of the apple tree.
   a. branch ✓
   b. leaf
   c. fruit

10. The slender boy was able to squeeze under the fence.
    a. chubby
    b. tall
    c. slim ✓

11. I wonder what is at the core of the earth.
    a. edge
    b. apple
    c. center ✓

12. He will call you anon in an hour.
    a. again
    b. tomorrow
    c. as soon as possible

88   Reading Mastery Plus, Level 6

Name _____

For items 13–53, circle the letter of the correct answer.

Lessons 31–40

13. Which character was a three-headed monster?
    a. Hades
    b. Cerberus ✓
    c. Zeus

14. How was the food that Persephone was used to different from Hades' food?
    a. She enjoyed fresh fruit and bread. ✓
    b. She did not like any foods.
    c. She liked richer foods.

15. What did seeing the magnificent flower make Demeter think?
    a. That Persephone had begun gardening
    b. That the sea nymphs had left the water
    c. That Persephone was in trouble ✓

16. Here's a fact: *My aunt wrote her autobiography last year.*
    Which one of the following items is relevant to the fact?
    a. My aunt's name is Sally.
    b. My aunt has had an interesting life. ✓
    c. We visited my aunt in Boston.

17. Here's a fact: *Chad won the 100-yard dash.*
    Which one of the following items is irrelevant to the fact?
    a. Chad has been practicing for months
    b. Chad is a sophomore this year. ✓
    c. Chad finished far ahead of the other runners.

18. Here's a main idea from *Sara Crewe: Sara's life changed entirely after she moved into the attic.*
    What is one supporting detail for that main idea?
    a. Nobody noticed her except to order her around. ✓
    b. She had a doll named Emily.
    c. The other students were rich.

Read the passage below. Then answer items 19–24.

Our story must now move out of Hades' dominions to observe what Demeter has been doing since her daughter was kidnapped. You will remember that we had a glimpse of her, half-hidden among the waving grain, while Persephone went swiftly whirling by in Hades' chariot. You will remember, too, the loud scream Persephone gave just when the chariot was out of sight.

Of all Persephone's outcries, this last shriek was the only one that reached Demeter's ears. She had mistaken the rumbling of the chariot wheels for a peal of thunder. She imagined a rain shower was coming and that it would help her make the corn grow.

At the sound of Persephone's shriek, Demeter looked about in every direction. She did not know where the shriek had come from, but she felt almost certain it was her daughter's voice.

It seemed unlikely that Persephone should have strayed over so many lands and seas. Nevertheless, Demeter decided to go home and assure herself that her daughter was safe.

Knowing that Persephone might be at the seashore, she hastened there as fast as she could. She soon beheld the wet faces of the poor sea nymphs peeping over a wave. These good creatures had been waiting on the sponge bank. Every minute or so, they popped their heads above water to see if Persephone had come back.

19. What did Demeter think the rumbling of the chariot wheels was?
    a. A rain shower
    b. A peal of thunder ✓
    c. Persephone's shriek

20. Why did Demeter decide to go home?
    a. She was finished working in the field.
    b. She wanted to assure herself that Persephone was safe. ✓
    c. She knew Persephone had been kidnapped.

Lesson 60 Test   89

21. Why did Demeter hurry to the seashore?

    Ⓐ She wanted to find out if Persephone was there.
    b. She didn't want Persephone to play with the nymphs.
    c. She needed to get back to her fields.

22. In which place would you find sand and shells?

    a. In Hades' chariot
    b. In Demeter's cornfield
    Ⓒ At the seashore

23. Why didn't Demeter follow the chariot?

    Ⓐ She didn't see where the chariot went.
    b. She knew Persephone wasn't in the chariot.
    c. She decided to keep working in the field.

24. What will Demeter probably do next?

    a. Make necklaces for the nymphs
    b. Show the nymphs how the shriek sounded
    Ⓒ Ask the sea nymphs if they've seen Persephone

Lessons 41–50

25. What creature did Sara and Erma feed from the garret window?

    a. A sparrow
    Ⓑ Melvin
    c. The monkey

26. Why did Sara give the beggar girl some buns from the bakery?

    a. The girl said she would repay Sara.
    Ⓑ Sara knew what it was like to be hungry.
    c. The bakery owner told her to.

27. Here is some evidence: *Some flowers have large, colorful petals. An orchid is a flower.*
So what do you know about orchids?

    Ⓐ Maybe orchids have large, colorful petals.
    b. Orchids have large, colorful petals.
    c. Orchids don't have large, colorful petals.

28. Here's a statement: *I'm so hungry I could eat a horse.*
What type of figurative language does that statement use?

    Ⓐ Exaggeration
    b. Metaphor
    c. Simile

29. Here's a statement: *Brent always runs the fifty-yard dash.*
Which one of the following items contradicts the statement?

    Ⓐ In his last race, Brent ran more than a mile.
    b. Brent practices running from our house to the corner.
    c. Brent's race was over in seconds.

30. Here is a statement. *I have never traveled outside the United States.*
Which one of the following items contradicts the statement?

    Ⓐ I had my picture taken beside the Eiffel Tower in Paris.
    b. Last summer, we vacationed in Oregon.
    c. The Grand Canyon is my favorite place.

Read the passage below. Then answer items 31–36.

He was really a very nice rat and did not mean the least harm. When he had stood on his hind legs and sniffed the air, with his bright eyes fixed on Sara, he had hoped she would understand this. When something inside him told him that Sara would not hurt him, he went softly toward the crumbs and began to eat them. As he ate, he glanced every now and then at Sara, just as the sparrows had done, and his expression touched her heart.

Sara sat and watched him without making any movement. One crumb was much larger than the others—in fact, it could scarcely be called a crumb. The rat wanted that piece very much, but it lay quite near the footstool, and he was still rather timid.

"I believe he wants it to carry to his family in the wall," Sara thought. "If I do not stir at all, perhaps he will come and get it."

Sara scarcely allowed herself to breathe, she was so deeply interested. The rat shuffled a little nearer and ate a few more crumbs; then he stopped and sniffed delicately. He gave a side glance at Sara and darted at the piece of bun just as the sparrow had earlier. The instant he had the bun, he fled back to the wall, slipped down a crack, and was gone.

31. What was the rat eating in Sara's room?

    a. Crumbs from Sara's toast
    b. Cookie crumbs
    Ⓒ Crumbs from a bun

32. Which one of the following events occurred last?

    a. The rat ate the crumbs.
    Ⓑ The rat fled through a crack in the wall.
    c. Sara sat without moving, watching the rat.

33. Why did the rat hesitate to come close to Sara?

    Ⓐ He was afraid she would hurt him.
    b. He had heard she was dangerous.
    c. He was afraid she had poisoned the crumbs.

34. What is the main idea of the passage?

    a. Sara thought the rat looked like a sparrow.
    Ⓑ The rat learned to trust Sara.
    c. Rats have a well-developed sense of smell.

35. What is one supporting idea for that main idea?

    Ⓐ Something inside the rat told him that Sara was a safe person.
    b. The rat sniffed delicately.
    c. Sara liked the rat's expression.

36. What will the rat probably do next?

    a. Try to get to the kitchen for larger crumbs
    b. Stay away from Sara's room
    Ⓒ Come back to Sara's room for more food

Lessons 51–60

37. Here is a statement from "The Tide Rises, the Tide Falls": *The little waves, with their soft white hands, efface the footprints in the sands.*
To what are the waves being compared?

    a. Clocks
    Ⓑ People
    c. Seaweed

38. In "The Necklace," how was Matilda different from her husband?

    a. She was very poor.
    b. She worked in a government office.
    Ⓒ She was not satisfied with what they had.

39. What is one thing Matilda probably did *not* learn from her experience?

    Ⓐ All diamonds are real.
    b. Be satisfied with what you have.
    c. Always tell the truth.

40. What color was the dress Miss Terwilliger wore to social functions?

    a. Shell pink
    b. Multicolored
    Ⓒ Robin's-egg blue

41. Which character mixes up his or her words?

    Ⓐ The sheriff
    b. Uncle Telly
    c. Miss Terwilliger

42. In "A White Heron," what was the main decision Sylvia had to make?

    a. Whether to stay with Mrs. Tilley
    b. How to spend the hundred dollars
    Ⓒ Whether to tell the hunter where the heron was

43. Why had Mrs. Tilley taken Sylvia in?

    a. She was paid a hundred dollars.
    Ⓑ Sylvia kept her from being lonely.
    c. She wanted a servant girl.

---

44. Here is one main idea from "A White Heron": *The young man has a collection of stuffed birds.*
What is one supporting detail for that main idea?

    a. The only bird he wants is the white heron.
    b. He is nice to young girls.
    Ⓒ He has dozens of preserved birds.

45. Here's a statement from "Written in March": *Like an army defeated the snow hath retreated.*
What type of figurative language does that statement use?

    a. Exaggeration
    Ⓑ Simile
    c. Metaphor

46. Here is some evidence: *Some boys with red hair are named Andrew. Andrew is a boy.*
So what do you know about Andrew?

    a. Andrew has red hair.
    Ⓑ Andrew might have red hair.
    c. Andrew doesn't have red hair.

47. How did you figure out the answer to item 46?

    Ⓐ By making a deduction
    b. By using words from the statement
    c. By looking in the answer key

Read the passage below. Then answer items 48–53.

One Sunday, Matilda took a walk to refresh herself from a hard week's work. She suddenly saw a woman leading a child. It was Mrs. Forester. She still looked young and beautiful and charming.

Matilda felt moved. Should she speak to Mrs. Forester? Yes, certainly. Now that Matilda had paid for the necklace, she would tell Mrs. Forester all about it. Why not?

She went up to her former friend.

"Hello, Mrs. Forester," she said.

Mrs. Forester did not recognize Matilda at all and stammered, "But . . . Madame . . . I do not know . . . you must be mistaken."

"No. I am Matilda Loisel."

Matilda's friend uttered a cry.

"Oh, my poor Matilda! You have changed so much!"

"Yes, I have had many hard days since I last saw you—and all because of you!"

"Of me! How so?"

"Do you remember that diamond necklace you loaned me to wear at the ball?"

"Yes. Well?"

"Well, I lost it."

"What do you mean? You brought it back."

"I brought you another one just like it. And we have been paying for it for ten years. It was not easy for us, because we had nothing. But at last it is over, and I am very glad."

Mrs. Forester's face seemed frozen.

"You say you purchased a necklace of diamonds to replace mine?"

"Yes. You never noticed it, then. They were very much alike."

And Matilda smiled with joy.

Mrs. Forester was deeply moved, and she took Matilda's two hands.

"Oh, my poor Matilda! Why, my necklace was fake! It was worth at most five hundred francs!"

48. Why did Mrs. Forester's face seem frozen?

    a. She was frightened by what Matilda told her.
    Ⓑ She realized that Matilda had made a terrible mistake.
    c. She felt very cold toward Matilda.

49. How did you figure out the answer to item 48?

    Ⓐ By making a deduction
    b. By using words from the passage
    c. By looking in the answer key

50. What will Mrs. Forester probably do next?

    Ⓐ Give Matilda the necklace
    b. Put the necklace in a safe
    c. Give Matilda five hundred francs

51. What mistake had Matilda made about the necklace she borrowed?

    Ⓐ She believed that it was made of real diamonds.
    b. She believed that it was a copy.
    c. She believed that it was beautiful.

---

52. Why did Matilda have to work so hard?

    a. She wanted to keep busy.
    Ⓑ She had to help pay for the necklace.
    c. Her husband was dead.

53. At first, why did Mrs. Forester say that she didn't know Matilda?

    a. She was embarrassed by Matilda.
    Ⓑ Matilda had changed so much.
    c. She wanted to keep the necklace.

STOP - end of test - SCORE: _____

Recording Individual Results

(Use the following script to record individual results.)

1. Look at your Individual Skills Profile Chart.
2. You're going to record your test results for lesson 60. First look at the test to find out which items you got wrong. Then circle those items on the chart.
3. Now record your results. I'll help you if you have any questions. (Circulate among the students as they record their results.)
4. (After the students finish, say:) Now count the items you did *not* circle and write the total in the **Total** box near the bottom of the column. The total should be the same as your test score.
5. Now you'll fill in the other boxes for lesson 60. If you scored 0 to 42 points, write an **X** in the box marked **Retest.** If you scored 43 to 53 points, write your score in the box marked **FINAL SCORE.**

Remedial Exercises

Students who scored 0 to 42 points on the test should be given remedial help. After the regular reading period is over, assemble these students and present the following exercises. The students will need their original test papers.

EXERCISE 1   Vocabulary Review

1. Let's talk about the meanings of some words.

2. The first words are **decked out.** When you are **decked out,** you are dressed up.
   • Everybody, what's another way of saying **We went to the prom dressed up**? (Signal.) *We went to the prom decked out.*

3. The next word is **obliged. Obliged** is another word for **required.**
   • Everybody, what's another way of saying **You are required to read ten pages**? (Signal.) *You are obliged to read ten pages.*

4. The next word is **frail. Frail** means "weak and delicate."
   • Everybody, what's another way of saying **The old man was weak and delicate**? (Signal.) *The old man was frail.*

5. The next word is **proposal.** When you make a **proposal,** you make a plan.
   • Everybody, what's another way of saying **You need to put your plan in writing**? (Signal.) *You need to put your proposal in writing.*

6. The next word is **incident. Incident** is another word for **event.**
   • Everybody, what's another way of saying **The event had a great effect on her life**? (Signal.) *The incident had a great effect on her life.*

7. The next word is **miscalculation.** To make a **miscalculation** is to make an error or a mistake.
   • Everybody, what's another way of saying **The clerk made a miscalculation in our bill**? (Signal.) *The clerk made an error in our bill.*

8. The next word is **endure.** When you tolerate a painful experience, you **endure** that experience.
   • Everybody, what's another way of saying **The brave woman tolerated her poverty**? (Signal.) *The brave woman endured her poverty.*

9. The next word is **maneuver.** A **maneuver** is a skillful movement.
   • Everybody, what's another way of saying **The dancer tried a new skillful movement**? (Signal.) *The dancer tried a new maneuver.*

10. The next word is **spurn. Spurn** is another word for **reject.**
    • Everybody, what's another way of saying **The publisher rejected the book he wrote**? (Signal.) *The publisher spurned the book he wrote.*

11. The next word is **reception.** A **reception** is a party that takes place after an important event.
    • Everybody, what's another way of saying **What will you wear to the party?** (Signal.) *What will you wear to the reception?*

12. The next word is **parasol**. A **parasol** is a light umbrella used for shade.
    - Everybody, what's another way of saying **Today is a good day for a light umbrella**? (Signal.) *Today is a good day for a parasol.*

13. The next word is **hostler**. A **hostler** is a person who takes care of horses or mules.
    - Everybody, what's another of saying **Who is the person who takes care of the horses here?** (Signal.) *Who is the hostler here?*

14. The next word is **efface**. When you **efface** something, you erase it.
    - Everybody, what's another way of saying **I will erase the chalk on the sidewalk?** (Signal.) *I will efface the chalk on the sidewalk.*

15. The next word is **reveal**. When you **reveal** something, you take it out of hiding and show it or tell about it.
    - Everybody, what's another way of saying **Please don't tell my secrets?** (Signal.) *Please don't reveal my secrets.*

16. The next word is **croon**. When you **croon**, you sing softly.
    - Everybody, what's another way of saying **Her grandfather loves to sing her a lullaby softly?** (Signal.) *Her grandfather loves to croon her a lullaby.*

17. The next word is **rare**. When something is **rare**, it is hard to find.
    - Everybody, what's another way of saying **Some kinds of butterflies are hard to find?** (Signal.) *Some kinds of butterflies are rare.*

18. The next word is **humiliating**. **Humiliating** means "quite embarrassing."
    - Everybody, what's another way of saying **It was quite embarrassing when I tripped on the stairs?** (Signal.) *It was quite humiliating when I tripped on the stairs.*

19. The next word is **gallant**. Someone who is **gallant** is brave and noble.
    - Everybody, what's another way of saying **The brave and noble knight won the hand of the beautiful princess?** (Signal.) *The gallant knight won the hand of the beautiful princess.*

20. The next word is **melancholy**. Someone who is **melancholy** is sad.
    - Everybody, what's another way of saying **That song always makes my sister feel sad?** (Signal.) *That song always makes my sister feel melancholy.*

21. The next word is **absurd**. When something is **absurd,** it is ridiculous.
    - Everybody, what's another way of saying **She always wears that ridiculous hat?** (Signal.) *She always wears that absurd hat.*

22. The next word is **bough**. A **bough** is a tree branch.
    - Everybody, what's another way of saying **The squirrel jumped onto a tree branch?** (Signal.) *The squirrel jumped onto a bough.*

23. The next word is **slender**. **Slender** is another word for **slim.**
    - Everybody, what's another way of saying **The slim woman tried to gain weight?** (Signal.) *The slender woman tried to gain weight.*

24. The next word is **core**. **Core** is another word for **center.**
    - Everybody, what's another way of saying **The core of the trouble was in the engine?** (Signal.) *The center of the trouble was in the engine.*

25. The last word is **anon. Anon** is an old word for **again.**
    - Everybody, what's an old way of saying **Please come anon?** (Signal.) *Please come again.*

EXERCISE 2   General Review

1. Who was Hades? (Idea: *The god of the underworld.*)
   - Who was Cerberus? (Idea: *Hades' dog.*)
   - Who was Zeus? (Idea: *The chief god.*)

2. What did Persephone like to eat? (Ideas: *Fresh fruit; bread.*)
   - What did Hades' cook feed her? (Ideas: *Rich pastry; highly seasoned meat; spiced sweetcakes.*)

3. Why did Persephone go into the fields? (Idea: *To gather flowers to make necklaces for the sea nymphs.*)
   - When she pulled on the magnificent flower, what happened? (Idea: *Hades and his golden chariot came out of the earth and carried her off.*)

4. Here's a fact: **The horse is loose.**
   - Here's some information: **The horse is brown.**
   - Is that information **relevant** or **irrelevant** to the fact? (Response: *Irrelevant.*)
   - Here's some more information: **The horse broke down the fence.**
   - Is that information **relevant** or **irrelevant** to the fact? (Response: *Relevant.*)

5. Here's a main idea from *Sara Crewe: Sara and Erma became good friends.*
   - Name some supporting details for that main idea. (Ideas: *Sara was drawn to the books Erma received; Sara helped Erma read the books; Erma was kind to Sara.*)

6. Who was Melvin? (Idea: *The rat that lived in the attic walls.*)
   - Who was the Lascar? (Idea: *The Indian Gentleman's servant.*)

7. Where was the beggar girl sitting? (Idea: *Outside the bakery.*)
   - What was she wearing? (Idea: *Rags.*)
   - When did she say was the last time she had eaten? (Idea: *She didn't know.*)
   - What was Sara going to buy with the money she had found? (Idea: *Buns.*)
   - Why? (Idea: *She was hungry.*)

8. Here is some evidence: **Some students are in math class. Maria is a student.**
   - So what do you know about Maria? (Idea: *She might be in math class.*)

9. What type of figurative language compares things by using the word *like*? (Response: *A simile.*)
   - What type of figurative language compares things without using the word *like*? (Response: *A metaphor.*)
   - What type of figurative language stretches the truth? (Response: *Exaggeration.*)

10. Here's a true statement: **James never plants flowers in his garden.**
    - Here's an item: **James put daisies around the tree in his garden.** Does that item contradict the true statement? (Response: *Yes.*)
    - Explain the contradiction. (Idea: *If James doesn't plant flowers in his garden, then he doesn't plant daisies.*)
    - Here's another item: **James put tomatoes in his garden.** Does that item contradict the true statement? (Response: *No.*)

11. What did Matilda think was important in life? (Ideas: *Gold dishes; fine food; fancy dresses; jewels.*)
    - What did her husband think she could wear to the grand ball? (Idea: *A dress she already had.*)

12. How did Matilda accept the responsibility of working to pay the debt? (Ideas: *Bravely; she resolved to work hard to help pay it.*)

13. What kind of classes did Miss Terwilliger teach? (Response: *Knitting.*)
    - What color was the dress she had knitted when she first started her classes? (Response: *Robin's-egg blue.*)

14. What was Uncle Telly's hobby? (Ideas: *Collecting string; making a huge ball of string.*)

15. Who entered the string-saver championship? (Response: *Uncle Telly, the sheriff, and Miss Terwilliger.*)

16. Why did Mrs. Tilley like Sylvia to be outdoors? (Ideas: *Sylvia loved the out-of-doors; Mrs. Tilley thought it was a good change for an orphan girl from the noisy, crowded town.*)

17. How did Sylvia feel about living at Mrs. Tilley's house? (Ideas: *She thought it was a beautiful place; she was happy to be away from mean children.*)

18. What did the young man offer for a white heron? (Response: *A hundred dollars.*)

19. What did Sylvia not understand about the young man? (Idea: *Why he killed birds when he liked them so much.*)

20. Here's a simile from "A White Heron": *To the creatures on the ground, her face was like a pale star.*
    • How could her face and a pale star be the same? (Ideas: *Both are visible and look white in the dark; both are high in the sky.*)
    • So what does the simile mean? (Idea: *Her face was bright and high in the sky.*)

21. Here is some evidence: **Some trees are evergreen. Mrs. Berlin has a tree in her yard.**
    • So what do you know about Mrs. Berlin's tree? (Idea: *It might be an evergreen.*)

EXERCISE 3   Passage Reading

Passage 1

1. Everybody, look at the passage on page 89 of your test. You're going to read the passage aloud.

2. (Call on individual students to read several sentences each. Correct any decoding errors. When the students finish, present the following questions.)

3. Why was Hades driving the chariot so fast? (Idea: *He had kidnapped Persephone.*)

4. What was making a noise on the road? (Idea: *The wheels.*)
    • What did it sound like? (Idea: *Thunder.*)

5. What kind of noise did Persephone make? (Idea: *A shriek.*)

6. What did Demeter think the noise was? (Idea: *Her daughter's voice.*)

7. What did Demeter do? (Ideas: *She went home; she went to the seashore to look for Persephone.*)

8. What were the sea nymphs doing? (Ideas: *Waiting on the sponge bank; watching for Persephone.*)

Passage 2

1. Everybody, look at the passage on pages 90 and 91 of your test. You're going to read the passage aloud.

2. (Call on individual students to read several sentences each. Correct any decoding errors. When the students finish, present the following questions.)

3. At the beginning of the passage, how is the rat described? (Idea: *As a very nice rat.*)

4. What did the rat want Sara to know? (Idea: *That he was harmless.*)

5. How did the rat approach the crumbs? (Idea: *Softly.*)

6. Did the rat gobble up the crumbs? (Response: *No.*)

7. Why did the rat hesitate to approach the largest crumb? (Idea: *He was timid.*)

8. How did he finally get the largest crumb? (Idea: *He looked sideways at Sara, then darted for the piece of bun and took it to his home in the wall.*)

Passage 3

1. Everybody, look at the passage on page 92 of your test. You're going to read the passage aloud.

2. (Call on individual students to read several sentences each. Correct any decoding errors. When the students finish, present the following questions.)

3. What did Matilda believe the necklace was made of? (Idea: *Real diamonds.*)
    • So what kind of necklace did Matilda buy to replace it? (Idea: *One with real diamonds.*)
    • How did Matilda help pay for the new necklace? (Idea: *By working hard.*)

4. Which character had changed a lot during the last ten years? (Response: *Matilda.*)
   - Which character had not changed much? (Response: *Mrs. Forester.*)

5. What did Mrs. Forester realize when Matilda told her about the necklace? (Idea: *That Matilda had made a mistake.*)

6. How can you tell that Mrs. Forester is a kind person? (Ideas: *She felt sorry for Matilda; she took Matilda's hands.*)
   - What could Mrs. Forester do to help Matilda now? (Ideas: *Give her the necklace; pay her back.*)

7. How much was the fake necklace worth? (Response: *Less than five hundred francs.*)
   - Do words in the passage say that the fake necklace "was worth less than five hundred francs"? (Response: *Yes.*)
   - Show me where. ✓
   - Do words in the passage say that Mrs. Forester was kind? (Response: *No.*)
   - How can you figure out that she's kind? (Idea: *By making a deduction.*)

Retesting the Students

After you've completed the remedial exercises, retest each student individually. To administer the retest, you will need the student's original test paper, a blank copy of the test, and a red pencil. Give the student the blank copy of the test. Say, "Look at page 88. You're going to take this test again. Read each item aloud and tell me the answer."

Use the student's original test paper to grade the retest. Use the red pencil to mark each correct answer with a **C** and each incorrect answer with an **X.** Then count one point for each correct answer and write the new score at the bottom of the page. Finally, revise the Individual Skills Profile Chart by drawing an **X** over any items the student missed on the retest.

Complete the Group Point Chart for lesson 60.

Administering the Checkouts

You can conduct checkouts by using the passage on page 92 of the Lesson 60 Mastery Test. See page 9 for a complete description of checkout procedures.

Tested Skills and Concepts

The Lesson 60 Mastery Test measures student mastery of the following skills and concepts.

- using vocabulary words in context (items 1–6)
- using context to predict word meaning (items 7–12)
- distinguishing characters by trait (items 13 and 41)
- making comparisons (items 14 and 38)
- evaluating problems and solutions (items 15 and 42)
- identifying relevant evidence (items 16 and 17)
- inferring details relevant to a main idea (items 18, 35, and 44)
- answering literal questions about a text (items 19 and 31)
- identifying literal cause and effect (items 20 and 52)
- interpreting a character's motives (item 21)
- distinguishing settings by features (item 22)
- inferring story details and events (item 23)
- predicting narrative outcomes (items 24 and 50)
- recalling details and events (items 25 and 40)
- interpreting a character's feelings (item 26)
- completing written deductions (items 27 and 46)
- interpreting figurative language (items 28, 37, and 45)
- identifying contradictions (items 29 and 30)
- sequencing narrative events (item 32)
- inferring causes and effects (items 33 and 48)
- inferring the main idea (item 34)
- predicting a character's actions (item 36)
- drawing conclusions (items 39 and 53)
- inferring a character's point of view (items 43 and 51)
- identifying inferential questions (items 47 and 49)

Lesson 70

Administering the Test

The Lesson 70 Mastery Test should be administered after the students complete all work on lesson 70 and before they begin work on lesson 71. Each student will need a pencil and a copy of the test. Use the following script.

1. (Have the students clear their desks. Make sure each student has a pencil.)
2. Now you're going to take another test on what you've learned. I'll give each of you a copy of the test. Don't begin until I tell you. (Pass out the tests.)
3. Write your name on the name line in the upper right-hand corner of each page.
4. Now you're ready to begin the test. Answer all the items on each page. There is no time limit. When you've finished, turn your test facedown and look up at me. Begin the test now. (If you are including the writing item as part of the testing session, tell students they can begin the writing item after they finish the mastery test.)

Grading the Test

You can grade the tests yourself, or you can have the students grade one another's tests. If you want the students to grade one another's tests, tell them to trade test papers. Then use the following script.

1. Now we're going to grade the test. I'll read the correct answer for each item. If the answer is correct, mark it with a **C**. If the answer is wrong, mark it with an **X**.
2. (Read the correct answers from the answer key on this page and the next.)
3. Now count the number of **correct** answers and enter the score at the end of the test.

Answer Key

Lesson 70

Name _____

For items 1–8, circle the letter of the answer that means the same thing as the underlined part.

1. The small and weak boy was no match for the bully.
   a. untidy
   b. puny ◯
   c. muffled

2. The colonies resisted the authority of England.
   a. rebelled against ◯
   b. sicced
   c. marred

3. A person with a lot of energy and ambition has spirit.
   a. loot
   b. bait
   c. spunk ◯

4. The rough weather made it difficult for the sailors.
   a. naval
   b. harsh ◯
   c. strained

5. Phil smiled at Rachel after she hailed him on the street.
   a. threw things at
   b. waved and shouted to ◯
   c. grabbed

6. The man was so stirred by the music that he began to weep.
   a. moved ◯
   b. annoyed
   c. deafened

7. The travelers visited all the principal places in the city.
   a. most royal
   b. most important ◯
   c. least interesting

8. The gale made us fearful that a hurricane was coming.
   a. strong wind ◯
   b. news report
   c. driving rain

For items 9–23, circle the letter of the correct answer.

9. Why did Frisco Kid keep a magazine page with a picture of a family on it?
   a. He imagined being in such a family. ◯
   b. He wanted to visit them when he returned to shore.
   c. He wanted to get married and have a family like that someday.

10. At the beginning of The Cruise of the Dazzler, why was Joe proud of his new life at sea?
   a. All his friends were becoming sailors.
   b. His mother wanted him to become a sailor.
   c. He wanted to show his father that he could take care of himself. ◯

11. In the following sentence, the star shows where a word is missing.
   *Three bottles were on the red shelf, but two * were on the floor.*
   What word is missing from the sentence?
   a. bottles ◯
   b. shelves
   c. floors

94 Reading Mastery Plus, Level 6

Name _____

12. In the following sentence, the star shows where a word is missing.
   *In our class, fourteen students are girls, and twelve * are boys.*
   What word is missing from the sentence?
   a. class
   b. girls
   c. students ◯

In the paragraph below, the sentences are numbered. Read the paragraph. Then answer items 13 and 14.

   (1) Ivan was talking about his car. (2) "My car is fantastic," he said. (3) "The body is rusted and the tires are bald."

13. Which sentence is an example of sarcasm?
   a. 1
   b. 2 ◯
   c. 3

14. Which sentence contradicts the sarcastic sentence?
   a. 1
   b. 2
   c. 3 ◯

In the passage below, the sentences are numbered. Read the passage. Then answer items 15–17.

   (1) "Hello, Jacob," said Ruth as she sat down next to him in the lunchroom. (2) The boy looked at her and removed his glasses. (3) "Aren't you talking to me?" she asked as she opened a carton of milk. (4) "Not here. (5) It's much too crowded." (6) "What do you mean?" (7) Zelda is the only other person at this table."

15. Which character says sentence 4?
   a. Jacob ◯
   b. Ruth
   c. Zelda

16. Which character says sentence 6?
   a. Jacob
   b. Ruth ◯
   c. Zelda

17. In sentence 5, what does the word it refer to?
   a. The school
   b. the lunchroom ◯
   c. Jacob's glasses

Read the passage below. Then answer items 18–23.

Joe heard a creaking noise in the night and saw the men hoisting the huge mainsail above him. Then Bill and Nick untied the *Dazzler* from the dock. The sloop soon caught the breeze and headed out into the bay, pulling a lifeboat and the skiff. Joe heard some talking in low tones. He heard someone say something about turning off the lights and keeping a sharp lookout, but he didn't know what to make of it.

The waterfront lights of Oakland began to slip by. A gentle north wind was blowing the sloop south, and the *Dazzler* sailed noiselessly through the water.

"Where are we going?" Joe asked Nick in a friendly tone.

"Oh, we're going to take a cargo from Bill's factory," Nick replied. Then Bill laughed as if he and Nick had a private joke. Joe didn't think Bill looked like a factory owner, but he said nothing.

Joe was sent into the cabin to blow out the cabin lamp. The *Dazzler* turned around and began to move toward the shore. Everybody kept silent except for occasional questions and answers between Bill and Pete. Finally, the sails were lowered cautiously.

Pete whispered to Frisco Kid, who went forward and dropped the anchor. Nick pulled the *Dazzler's* lifeboat and his skiff alongside the sloop. Bill and Nick got into the skiff, and Bill said, "Make sure you keep quiet."

Then Frisco Kid motioned Joe to get into the *Dazzler's* lifeboat. "Can you row?" Frisco Kid asked. Joe nodded his head yes. "Then take these oars," Frisco Kid continued, "and don't make a racket."

Lesson 70 Test 95

Lesson 70 35

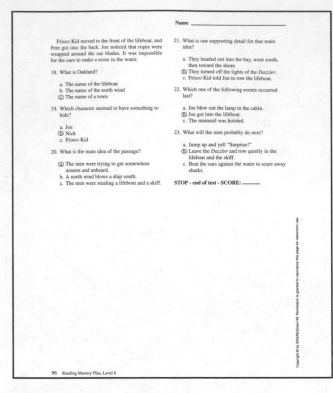

Name _____

Frisco Kid moved to the front of the lifeboat, and Pete got into the back. Joe noticed that ropes were wrapped around the oar blades. It was impossible for the oars to make a noise in the water.

18. What is Oakland?

   a. The name of the lifeboat
   b. The name of the north wind
   ⓒ The name of a town

19. Which character seemed to have something to hide?

   a. Joe
   ⓑ Nick
   c. Frisco Kid

20. What is the main idea of the passage?

   ⓐ The men were trying to get somewhere unseen and unheard.
   b. A north wind blows a ship south.
   c. The men were stealing a lifeboat and a skiff.

21. What is one supporting detail for that main idea?

   a. They headed out into the bay, went south, then toward the shore.
   ⓑ They turned off the lights of the *Dazzler.*
   c. Frisco Kid told Joe to row the lifeboat.

22. Which one of the following events occurred last?

   a. Joe blew out the lamp in the cabin.
   ⓑ Joe got into the lifeboat.
   c. The mainsail was hoisted.

23. What will the men probably do next?

   a. Jump up and yell "Surprise!"
   ⓑ Leave the *Dazzler* and row quietly in the lifeboat and the skiff.
   c. Beat the oars against the water to scare away sharks.

STOP - end of test - SCORE: _____

96   Reading Mastery Plus, Level 6

Recording Individual Results

(Use the following script to record individual results.)

1. Look at your Individual Skills Profile Chart.
2. You're going to record your test results for lesson 70. First look at the test to find out which items you got wrong. Then circle those items on the chart.
3. Now record your results. I'll help you if you have any questions. (Circulate among the students as they record their results.)
4. (After the students finish, say:) Now count the items you did *not* circle and write the total in the **Total** box near the bottom of the column. The total should be the same as your test score.
5. Now you'll fill in the other boxes for lesson 70. If you scored 0 to 18 points, write an **X** in the box marked **Retest.** If you scored 19 to 23 points, write your score in the box marked **FINAL SCORE.**

Remedial Exercises

Students who scored 0 to 18 points on the test should be given remedial help. After the regular reading period is over, assemble these students and present the following exercises. The students will need their original test papers.

EXERCISE 1   Vocabulary Review

1. Let's talk about the meanings of some words.

2. The first word is **untidy.** Something that is messy and disordered is **untidy.**
   • Everybody, what's another way of saying **His room was messy and disordered**? (Signal.) *His room was untidy.*

3. The next word is **puny.** Something that is small and weak is **puny.**
   • Everybody, what's another way of saying **The kitten was small and weak**? (Signal.) *The kitten was puny.*

4. The next word is **muffled.** Sounds that are **muffled** are softened or deadened.
   • Everybody, what's another way of saying **His voice was softened by the scarf over his mouth**? (Signal.) *His voice was muffled by the scarf over his mouth.*

5. The next word is **rebel.** When you **rebel,** you resist doing something.
   • Everybody, what's another way of saying **Why did you resist my rules? (Signal.)** *Why did you rebel against my rules?*

6. The next word is **sic.** When you **sic** an animal, you order the animal to attack somebody.
   • Everybody, what's another way of saying **It is cruel to order a dog to attack a small animal**? (Signal.) *It is cruel to sic a dog on a small animal.*

7. The next word is **mar.** Another word for **mar** is **ruin.**
   • Everybody, what's another way of saying **Dragging the sofa will ruin the floor**? (Signal.) *Dragging the sofa will mar the floor.*

8. The next word is **loot. Loot** is stolen material.
   • Everybody, what's another way of saying **The thieves were arguing over the stolen material**? (Signal.) *The thieves were arguing over the loot.*

9. The next word is **bait. Bait** is anything that lures a person or an animal into a trap.
   - Everybody, what's another way of saying **Will you put the lure on my fishing line?** (Signal.) *Will you put the bait on my fishing line?*

10. The next word is **spunk.** When you have **spunk,** you have spirit and determination.
    - Everybody, what's another way of saying **Our cheerleaders have a lot of spirit?** (Signal.) *Our cheerleaders have a lot of spunk.*

11. The next word is **naval.** When something is **naval,** it belongs to the navy.
    - Everybody, what's another way of saying **We toured the base that belongs to the navy?** (Signal.) *We toured the naval base.*

12. The next word is **harsh.** Harsh means "rough" or "unpleasant."
    - Everybody, what's another way of saying **We had a rough winter?** (Signal.) *We had a harsh winter.*

13. The next word is **strained. Strained** is another word for **tense.**
    - Everybody, what's another way of saying **Our meeting with the principal was tense?** (Signal.) *Our meeting with the principal was strained.*

14. The next word is **hail. Hail** means "to summon by calling out."
    - Everybody, what's another way of saying **Have you ever summoned a taxi by calling out?** (Signal.) *Have you ever hailed a taxi?*

15. The next word is **stir. Stir** means "to produce strong emotion."
    - Everybody, what's another way of saying **The story of the orphan created strong emotion in him?** (Signal.) *The story of the orphan stirred him.*

16. The next word is **principal. Principal** means "main" or "most important."
    - Everybody, what's another way of saying **Myong is the most important character in the play?** (Signal.) *Myong is the principal character in the play.*

17. The last word is **gale.** A **gale** is a strong wind.
    - Everybody, what's another way of saying **The recent strong wind blew down many trees?** (Signal.) *The recent gale blew down many trees.*

EXERCISE 2   General Review

1. What did Frisco Kid have as a substitute for a real family? (Idea: *A picture of a family from a magazine.*)
   - What did he think about the family in the picture? (Ideas: *The picture made him realize he was lonely; after a while, the family seemed real to him; he imagined what they would think of him, and that made him want to be a better person.*)

2. What did Joe think his friends would say when they heard he had gone to sea? (Idea: *He thought they would be impressed.*)
   - How did he think his mother would react? (Idea: *He thought she would worry.*)
   - How did he feel about his father? (Ideas: *He felt his father didn't understand boys; he wanted to prove to his father that boys had some rights; he wanted to prove he could take care of himself.*)

3. Here's a sentence: *Hector was happy, but Maria wasn't happy.*
   - Here's the same sentence with a word missing: *Hector was happy, but Maria wasn't.*
   - What word is missing from that sentence? (Response: *Happy.*)

4. Sometimes people say the opposite of what they really mean. What is the word for that type of figurative language? (Response: *Sarcasm.*)

5. Everybody, look at the passage near the bottom of the left column on page 95 of your test. (Call on a student to read the passage aloud.)
   - Which character says sentence 7? (Response: *Ruth.*)
   - Which character says sentence 5? (Response: *Jacob.*)
   - In sentence 3, to whom does the word *she* refer? (Response: *Ruth.*)

EXERCISE 3   Passage Reading

1. Everybody, look at the passage in the right column on page 95 of your test. You're going to read the passage aloud.

2. (Call on individual students to read several sentences each. Correct any decoding errors. When the students finish, present the following questions.)

3. When the *Dazzler* left the dock, what was it pulling? (Idea: *A lifeboat and the skiff.*)

4. Name some things the men did so that they would not be seen or heard. (Ideas: *Turned off the lights; blew out the cabin lamp; kept silent; wrapped the oars.*)

5. Why did they do these things? (Idea: *So that people on the shore wouldn't know they were heading there.*)

6. What seems to be their plan? (Idea: *Stealing.*)

7. How do they plan to get to shore? (Idea: *By leaving the* Dazzler *anchored and rowing the lifeboat and the skiff to shore.*)

8. What people are in the lifeboat? (Idea: *Frisco Kid, Pete, and Joe.*)
   - What people are in the skiff? (Idea: *Bill and Nick.*)

9. Why didn't Joe ask more questions after he asked Nick where they were going? (Ideas: *He thought Nick and Bill didn't want him to know what they were doing; everyone was quiet, and Bill told Joe to be quiet.*)

10. What was wrapped around the oars to keep them quiet? (Response: *Ropes.*)

Retesting the Students

After you have completed the remedial exercises, retest each student individually. To administer the retest, you will need the student's original test paper, a blank copy of the test, and a red pencil. Give the student a blank copy of the test. Say, "Look at page 94. You're going to take this test again. Read each item aloud and tell me the answer."

Use the student's original test paper to grade the retest. Use the red pencil to mark each correct answer with a **C** and each incorrect answer with an **X.** Then count one point for each correct answer and write the new score at the bottom of the page. Finally, revise the Individual Skills Profile Chart by drawing an **X** over any items the student missed on the retest.

Complete the Group Point Chart for lesson 70.

Administering the Checkouts

You can conduct checkouts by using the passage on page 95 of the Lesson 70 Mastery Test. See page 9 for a complete description of checkout procedures.

Tested Skills and Concepts

The Lesson 70 Mastery Test measures student mastery of the following skills and concepts.

- using vocabulary words in context (items 1-4)
- using context to predict word meaning (items 5-8)
- interpreting a character's motives (item 9)
- inferring a character's point of view (item 10)
- interpreting shortened sentences (items 11 and 12)
- interpreting figurative language (item 13)
- identifying contradictions (item 14)
- interpreting extended dialogues (items 15 and 16)
- interpreting substitute words (item 17)
- inferring story details and events (item 18)
- distinguishing characters by trait (item 19)
- inferring the main idea (item 20)
- inferring details relevant to a main idea (item 21)
- sequencing narrative events (item 22)
- predicting narrative outcomes (item 23)

Lesson 80

Administering the Test

The Lesson 80 Mastery Test should be administered after the students complete all work on lesson 80 and before they begin work on lesson 81. Each student will need a pencil and a copy of the test. Use the following script.

1. (Have the students clear their desks. Make sure each student has a pencil.)
2. Now you're going to take another test on what you've learned. I'll give each of you a copy of the test. Don't begin until I tell you. (Pass out the tests.)
3. Write your name on the name line in the upper right-hand corner of each page.
4. Now you're ready to begin the test. Answer all the items on each page. There is no time limit. When you've finished, turn your test facedown and look up at me. Begin the test now. (If you are including the writing item as part of the testing session, tell students they can begin the writing item after they finish the mastery test.)

Grading the Test

You can grade the tests yourself, or you can have the students grade one another's tests. If you want the students to grade one another's tests, tell them to trade test papers. Then use the following script.

1. Now we're going to grade the test. I'll read the correct answer for each item. If the answer is correct, mark it with a **C**. If the answer is wrong, mark it with an **X**.
2. (Read the correct answers from the answer key on this page and the next.)
3. Now count the number of **correct** answers and enter the score at the end of the test.

Answer Key

Lesson 80　　　Name _____

For items 1–8, circle the letter of the answer that means the same thing as the underlined part.

1. After several days, the climbers reached the top of the mountain.
   a. summit
   b. licking
   c. vengeance

2. Ted really hated carrots and peas.
   a. writhed
   b. snickered
   c. despised

3. His greeting to me was warm and sincere.
   a. reception
   b. fit
   c. vengeance

4. The cheerleader was balanced on her teammate's shoulders.
   a. unheeded
   b. poised
   c. scornful

5. The football team forged ahead when they got the ball.
   a. went the wrong direction
   b. moved forward powerfully
   c. eased toward the goal slowly and cautiously

6. Her voice teacher said she shows promise to be a singer.
   a. doesn't really want
   b. vows
   c. shows talent to learn

7. We toured a plantation where cotton is grown.
   a. large farm
   b. greenhouse
   c. plowed field

8. The ruts in the road made our trip bumpy.
   a. rocks
   b. grooves
   c. painted lines

For items 9–24, circle the letter of the correct answer.

9. Here's a sentence that combines two short sentences: *That watch is made with platinum, an expensive metal.*
   The first short sentence is *That watch is made with platinum.*
   What is the second short sentence?
   a. That watch is an expensive metal.
   b. That watch is expensive.
   c. Platinum is an expensive metal.

10. Here's a fact: *The car screeched to a halt.*
    Which one of the following items is relevant to the fact?
    a. The driver saw a dog running across the road.
    b. The car was red and had whitewall tires.
    c. The driver was listening to rock music.

11. Here's an exaggeration from "Casey at the Bat": *And then when Cooney died at first, and Barrows did the same. . . ."*
    What did Cooney and Barrows actually do?
    a. Passed away on first base
    b. Got thrown out at first base
    c. Got hit hard with a ball at first base

12. Here's one main idea from the Harriet Tubman biography: *At the beginning of the story, Jim was a slave.*
    What is one supporting detail for that main idea?
    a. He went to a train station.
    b. He lived on a plantation.
    c. He moved to Canada.

Lesson 80 Test　97

Name _____

13. Which of the following states was a slave state?
    a. Maryland
    b. New York
    c. Pennsylvania

14. What was the trail of hiding places called that led runaway slaves to the North?
    a. The Trail of Tears
    b. The Northern Connection
    c. The Underground Railroad

15. Why was there a reward for Harriet Tubman's capture?
    a. She knew how to read, and slaves weren't allowed to learn to read.
    b. She helped runaway slaves.
    c. She had sleeping fits, and people thought they were contagious.

Read the paragraph below. Then answer items 16–18.

By the time the ferry reached the shore, the people had become like wild animals. They poured off the ferry and ran toward the police station. The police shot into the crowd. Two men were wounded, but the mob continued with more determination than ever.

16. What is the main idea of the paragraph?
    a. The people traveled on a ferry to the police station.
    b. The police had guns.
    c. The people on the ferry were angry.

17. How did you figure out the answer to item 16?
    a. By making a deduction
    b. By looking in the answer key
    c. By using words from the passage

18. Which one of the following events occurred first?
    a. The people ran toward the police station.
    b. The ferry arrived at the dock.
    c. The police shot two men.

Read the passage below. Then answer items 19–24.

Frisco Kid, Pete, and Joe clung to the *Dazzler*, which was in danger of sinking at any moment. Meanwhile, Nelson turned the *Reindeer* around and came back toward the *Dazzler*.

"Ze wild man! Ze wild man!" Pete shrieked, watching the maneuver in amazement. "He wants us to jump on his sloop. He thinks he can turn around in this gale! He will die! We will all die! Oh, ze fool! Ze fool!"

But Nelson tried the impossible. At the right moment, he turned the *Reindeer* around and hauled back toward the *Dazzler*.

"Here she comes! Get ready to jump!" Pete cried. But Frisco Kid and Joe only looked at each other. They said nothing, but they both sensed that they should stay with the *Dazzler* and rescue the safe.

The *Reindeer* dashed by them again. She was so close that it appeared she would run them down. Pete was the only one to jump. He sprang for the *Reindeer* like a cat and caught onto the railing with both hands. Then the *Reindeer* forged ahead. Pete clung to the railing and worked his way up until he dropped onto the deck.

And then, to Joe's amazement, the *Reindeer* turned around again. She plowed back toward the *Dazzler* at breakneck speed. She was tilted at such an angle that it seemed she would sink.

Just then, the storm burst in fury, and the shouting wind made the sea churn. The *Reindeer* dipped from view behind an immense wave. The wave rolled on, but the boys could see only the angry waters where the *Reindeer* had been. They looked a second time. There was no *Reindeer*. They were alone on the ocean.

19. Why was Joe so amazed when the *Reindeer* turned around for the last time?
    a. The men were trying to sink the *Dazzler*.
    b. The men were trying to save his life.
    c. The storm was the worst he had ever experienced.

98　Reading Mastery Plus, Level 6

Lesson 80　　39

Name _____

20. What happened to the *Reindeer* at the end of the passage?

   a. The wave carried her far away from the *Dazzler.*
   (b) She sank to the bottom of the ocean.
   c. She tipped over on her side.

21. Why did Joe stay on board the *Dazzler?*

   a. He was afraid to jump onto the *Reindeer.*
   (b) He wanted to rescue the safe.
   c. He knew the *Reindeer* would sink.

22. What will Joe and Frisco Kid probably do next?

   a. Jump overboard and swim for shore
   b. Try to find the *Reindeer*
   (c) Try to fix the *Dazzler*

23. How was Joe different from Pete?

   (a) Joe thought the safe was important.
   b. Joe was in great danger.
   c. Joe was on board the *Dazzler.*

24. One sentence says "... the shouting wind made the sea churn." What type of figurative language does that sentence use?

   a. Simile
   (b) Metaphor
   c. Exaggeration

STOP - end of test - SCORE: _____

Lesson 80 Test 99

Recording Individual Results

(Use the following script to record individual results.)

1. Look at your Individual Skills Profile Chart.
2. You're going to record your test results for lesson 80. First look at the test to find out which items you got wrong. Then circle those items on the chart.
3. Now record your results. I'll help you if you have any questions. **(Circulate among the students as they record their results.)**
4. **(After the students finish, say:)** Now count the items you did *not* circle and write the total in the **Total** box near the bottom of the column. The total should be the same as your test score.
5. Now you'll fill in the other boxes for lesson 80. If you scored 0 to 19 points, write an **X** in the box marked **Retest.** If you scored 20 to 24 points, write your score in the box marked **FINAL SCORE.**

Remedial Exercises

Students who scored 0 to 19 points on the test should be given remedial help. After the regular reading period is over, assemble these students and present the following exercises. The students will need their original test papers.

EXERCISE 1   Vocabulary Review

1. Let's talk about the meanings of some words.

2. The first word is **summit.** The **summit** of something is the top of that thing.
   • Everybody, what's another way of saying **They climbed to the top of the mountain**? (Signal.) *They climbed to the summit of the mountain.*

3. The next word is **licking.** A **licking** is a beating.
   • Everybody, what's another way of saying **Our team got quite a beating from the Warriors**? (Signal.) *Our team got quite a licking from the Warriors.*

4. The next word is **vengeance. Vengeance** is another word for **revenge.**
   • Everybody, what's another way of saying **Is it wise to try to get revenge?** (Signal.) *Is it wise to try to get vengeance?*

5. The next word is **writhe.** When something **writhes,** it twists and turns.
   • Everybody, what's another way of saying **The injured person twisted and turned with pain**? (Signal.) *The injured person writhed with pain.*

6. The next word is **snicker.** When you **snicker,** you hide your laughter.
   • Everybody, what's another way of saying **Were you hiding your laughter at her mistake?** (Signal.) *Were you snickering at her mistake?*

7. The next word is **despise.** When you **despise** something, you really hate it.
   • Everybody, what's another way of saying **She really hated traveling by bus**? (Signal.) *She despised traveling by bus.*

8. The next word is **reception.** One meaning of **reception** is "greeting."
   • Everybody, what's another way of saying **Please give our guests a pleasant greeting**? (Signal.) *Please give our guests a pleasant reception.*

9. The next word is **fit.** A **fit** is an attack brought on by a disease.
   - Everybody, what's another way of saying **I took medicine for my coughing attack**? (Signal.) *I took medicine for my coughing fit.*

10. The next word is **unheeded.** When something is **unheeded,** nobody pays attention to it.
    - Everybody, what's another way of saying **Nobody paid attention to the tornado warning**? (Signal.) *The tornado warning was unheeded.*

11. The next word is **poised. Poised** is another word for **balanced.**
    - Everybody, what's another way of saying **The ballerina is balanced on her toes**? (Signal.) *The ballerina is poised on her toes.*

12. The next word is **scornful.** When something is **scornful,** it is full of disrespect and dislike.
    - Everybody, what's another way of saying **The rude comment was full of disrespect**? (Signal.) *The rude comment was scornful.*

13. The next term is **forge ahead.** When you **forge ahead,** you move forward powerfully.
    - Everybody, what's another way of saying **The ship moved forward powerfully through the rough seas**? (Signal.) *The ship forged ahead through the rough seas.*

14. The next term is **show promise.** When you **show promise,** you show talent in something.
    - Everybody, what's another way of saying **Harry shows a lot of talent in tennis**? (Signal.) *Harry shows a lot of promise in tennis.*

15. The next word is **plantation.** A **plantation** is a large farm.
    - Everybody, what's another way of saying **Have you ever seen a large farm where tobacco is grown**? (Signal.) *Have you ever seen a plantation where tobacco is grown?*

16. The last word is **ruts. Ruts** are grooves or tracks in a road, especially a dirt road.
    - Everybody, what's another way of saying **The large trucks made grooves in the road**? (Signal.) *The large trucks made ruts in the road.*

EXERCISE 2   General Review

1. Here's a sentence that contains a new word: **The explorer wore mukluks.**
   - What is the new word? (Response: *Mukluks.*)
   - Here's a sentence that tells the meaning of the new word: **Mukluks are a kind of boot.**
   - Combine the sentences so that the meaning comes after the new word. (Response: *The explorer wore mukluks, a kind of boot.*)

2. Here's a fact: **The boy closed the book.**
   - Here's an item: **The boy had just finished reading the book.**
   - Does that item help explain the fact? (Response: *Yes.*)
   - So is that item **relevant** or **irrelevant**? (Response: *Relevant.*)

3. Here's an exaggeration: **There were a million people at our house last night.**
   - Could a million people really fit into a house? (Response: *No.*)
   - How many people were really in the house? (Idea: *A large number.*)

4. Here's a main idea from "Harriet Tubman": **The life of a slave was very harsh.**
   - Name some supporting details for that main idea. (Ideas: *Slaves could be sold away from their families; their work was physically difficult; they were sometimes beaten; sometimes they weren't given enough food; they weren't allowed to learn to read.*)

5. Why was Harriet Tubman wanted? (Ideas: *She was a runaway slave; she helped other runaway slaves escape.*)

6. As the runaway slaves traveled north to freedom, where would they stay during the day? (Idea: *In the homes of people who helped them.*)
   - What were the guides called who led the runaways from one hiding place to the next? (Response: *Conductors.*)

7. What was the amount of the reward for Harriet Tubman's capture? (Response: *Five thousand dollars, and, later, ten thousand.*)

8. Everybody, look at the paragraph in the left column on page 98 of your test. (Call on a student to read the paragraph aloud.)
   • Who are the main characters in the paragraph? (Ideas: *A mob of people; the police.*)
   • What is the main thing the people did? (Idea: *Angrily went to the police station.*)
   • So what is the main idea of the paragraph? (Idea: *The mob angrily went to the police station.*)

EXERCISE 3   Passage Reading

1. Everybody, look at the passage in the right column on page 98 of your test. You're going to read the passage aloud.

2. (Call on individual students to read several sentences each. Correct any decoding errors. When the students finish, present the following questions.)

3. Why did the men turn the *Reindeer* around after they picked up Pete? (Idea: *They wanted to save Frisco Kid and Joe.*)
   • What could the men have done instead? (Ideas: *Forgotten about the boys; kept on sailing.*)

4. Why did the *Reindeer* disappear? (Idea: *It sank.*)

5. What did Joe and Frisco Kid want to rescue on the *Dazzler?* (Idea: *The safe.*)
   • So what did they do when the *Reindeer* went by? (Idea: *Stayed on the* Dazzler.)
   • What will they do now that the *Reindeer* has sunk? (Ideas: *Try to rescue the safe; try to fix the* Dazzler.)

6. What did Pete think was more important, the safe or his life? (Response: *His life.*)
   • So what did he do when the *Reindeer* went by? (Idea: *Jumped onto it.*)

7. What kind of figurative language compares things by using the word *like?* (Response: *A simile.*)
   • What kind of figurative language compares things without using the word *like?* (Response: *A metaphor.*)
   • What kind of figurative language stretches the truth? (Response: *Exaggeration.*)

Retesting the Students

After you've completed the remedial exercises, retest each student individually. To administer the retest, you will need the student's original test paper, a blank copy of the test, and a red pencil. Give the student the blank copy of the test. Say, "Look at page 97. You're going to take this test again. Read each item aloud and tell me the answer."

Use the student's original test paper to grade the retest. Use the red pencil to mark each correct answer with a **C** and each incorrect answer with an **X.** Then count one point for each correct answer and write the new score at the bottom of the page. Finally, revise the Individual Skills Profile Chart by drawing an **X** over any items the student missed on the retest.

Complete the Group Point Chart for lesson 80.

Administering the Checkouts

You can conduct checkouts by using the passage on page 98 of the Lesson 80 Mastery Test. See page 9 for a complete description of checkout procedures.

Tested Skills and Concepts

The Lesson 80 Mastery Test measures student mastery of the following skills and concepts.

- using vocabulary words in context (items 1–4)
- using context to predict word meaning (items 5–8)
- interpreting combined sentences (item 9)
- identifying relevant evidence (item 10)
- interpreting figurative language (items 11 and 24)
- inferring details relevant to a main idea (item 12)
- distinguishing settings by features (item 13)
- recalling details and events (item 14)
- drawing conclusions (item 15)
- inferring the main idea (item 16)
- identifying inferential questions (item 17)
- sequencing narrative events (item 18)
- interpreting a character's feelings (item 19)
- inferring story details and events (item 20)
- interpreting a character's motives (item 21)
- predicting a character's actions (item 22)
- making comparisons (item 23)

Lesson 90

Administering the Test

The Lesson 90 Mastery Test should be administered after the students complete all work on lesson 90 and before they begin work on lesson 91. Each student will need a pencil and a copy of the test. Use the following script.

1. (Have the students clear their desks. Make sure each student has a pencil.)
2. Now you're going to take another test on what you've learned. This test will be longer than the others you've taken because it has questions about the last thirty lessons. I'll give each of you a copy of the test. Don't begin until I tell you. (Pass out the tests.)
3. Write your name on the name line in the upper right-hand corner of each page.
4. Now you're ready to begin the test. Answer all the items on each page. There is no time limit. When you've finished, turn your test facedown and look up at me. Begin the test now. (If you are including the writing item as part of the testing session, tell students they can begin the writing item after they finish the mastery test.)

Grading the Test

You can grade the tests yourself, or you can have the students grade one another's tests. If you want the students to grade one another's tests, tell them to trade test papers. Then use the following script.

1. Now we're going to grade the test. I'll read the correct answer for each item. If the answer is correct, mark it with a **C**. If the answer is wrong, mark it with an **X**.
2. (Read the correct answers from the answer key on this page and the next.)
3. Now count the number of **correct** answers and enter the score at the end of the test.

Answer Key

Lesson 90

Name _____

For items 1–12, circle the letter of the answer that means the same thing as the underlined part.

1. The sailors went below to the cabin where they slept for the night.

   a. quarantine station
   b. skiff
   c. forecastle

2. Did the two cars run into each other in the intersection?

   a. collide
   b. churn
   c. hurtle

3. The quarterback used trickery to fool the other team into thinking he was going left.

   a. junction
   b. deception
   c. agony

4. Carrying the large and heavy sofa was difficult.

   a. supernatural
   b. plush
   c. bulky

5. We enjoyed the old story about Johnny Appleseed.

   a. sensation
   b. legend
   c. exception

6. Please meet me before class so we can study for the test.

   a. beforehand
   b. systematically
   c. dryly

7. She defied her sergeant's orders to run laps.

   a. waited for
   b. applauded
   c. challenged

8. She gave me a smirk when she won the bet.

   a. mocking smile
   b. handshake
   c. five-dollar bill

9. Ferdinand walked down the long hotel corridor looking for the door to his room.

   a. lobby
   b. hallway
   c. parking lot

10. Sophia is in debt after buying a car.

    a. owes money
    b. is having a great time
    c. is entering car races

11. Our grandfathers were in the same regiment in the Korean War.

    a. boot camp
    b. airplane
    c. army unit

12. I was dumbfounded when I won the prize.

    a. briefly astonished
    b. lightheaded
    c. in a coma

100 Reading Mastery Plus, Level 6

Name _____

For items 13–53, circle the letter of the correct answer.

Lessons 61–70

13. If you want to find out where Henry Ford was born, which reference book would you use?

    a. Atlas
    b. Encyclopedia
    c. Dictionary

14. There's a statement: The enemy's guns sounded like soldiers marching. What type of figurative language does that statement use?

    a. Metaphor
    b. Simile
    c. Exaggeration

15. Here's a statement: You really did a great job of doing the dishes. There's water all over the floor. The countertops are greasy. This bowl still has cereal stuck to it. What type of figurative language does that statement use?

    a. Metaphor
    b. Exaggeration
    c. Sarcasm

16. Here's a statement: The daffodils danced in the breeze. What type of figurative language does that statement use?

    a. Metaphor
    b. Exaggeration
    c. Sarcasm

Look at the map below. Then answer items 17–19.

17. In which state is St. Louis?

    a. Arkansas
    b. Iowa
    c. Missouri

18. Which city borders on the Gulf of Mexico?

    a. Minneapolis
    b. New Orleans
    c. Memphis

19. Which one of the following statements contradicts the map?

    a. Memphis is north of New Orleans.
    b. Iowa is south of Missouri.
    c. New Orleans is south of Arkansas.

Lesson 90 Test 101

Lesson 90 45

Read the passage below. Then answer items 20–24.

Joe dashed out into the water for the lifeboat. Pete and Frisco Kid had the boat's nose pointed out to sea and were calmly awaiting Joe's arrival. They had their oars all ready for the start, but they held them quietly at rest. The other skiff was still on the beach. Bill was trying to shove it off and was calling on Nick to lend a hand. But Nick had lost his head completely and came floundering through the water toward the lifeboat.

Joe climbed into the heavily loaded lifeboat, and Nick followed him. Nick's extra weight nearly sank the lifeboat. In the meantime, the two men on the beach had pulled out pistols and opened fire. The alarm had spread. Voices and cries could be heard from the ships on the pier. In the distance, a police siren blew frantically.

"Get out!" Frisco Kid shouted at Nick. "You ain't going to sink us. Go and help your partner!"

But Nick's teeth were chattering with fright, and he did not move or speak.

"Throw the crazy man out!" Pete ordered. At this moment, a bullet shattered Pete's oar, and he coolly proceeded to look for a spare one.

"Give us a hand, Joe," Frisco Kid commanded.

Joe understood, and together they seized Nick and flung him overboard. Two or three bullets splashed about him as he came to the surface just in time to be picked up by Bill, who had at last succeeded in getting the skiff into the water. A few oar strokes into the darkness quickly took them out of range of the pistols.

20. Into which boat did Nick climb?

a. The *Dazzler*
(b) The lifeboat
c. The skiff

21. Which man did Pete order the boys to throw out?

a. Joe
b. Bill
(c) Nick

22. Which character was panicking?

a. Pete
(b) Nick
c. Frisco Kid

23. Why were the police shooting at the boats?

a. They were target shooting, and the boats were the targets.
b. They were trying to scare away the men.
(c) They didn't want the men to escape.

24. In the sentence in the last paragraph that begins "Two or three bullets splashed about him as he came to the surface . . . ," to which person does *him* refer?

a. Frisco Kid
b. Joe
(c) Nick

Lessons 71–80

25. In the Harriet Tubman biography, which of the following events occurred last?

(a) Harriet pretended to read a book on the train.
b. Jim was beaten when the horse broke its leg.
c. The slaves hid under a pile of laundry in a wagon.

26. How was being a free man different from being a slave?

a. There weren't any differences.
b. A free man had food, clothing, and shelter.
(c) A free man could own property.

27. In the following sentence, the star shows where a word is missing.
*Most students were in the classroom, but some * were on the playground.*
What word is missing from the sentence?

a. classrooms
b. playgrounds
(c) students

In the passage below, the sentences are numbered. Read the passage. Then answer items 28–30.

(1) "Hi, Matt," said Emily as she came onto the tennis court.
(2) The boy was swinging his racket as if he were hitting a tennis ball.
(3) "Are you ready to play?" she asked as she laced up her shoes.
(4) "Yes. (5) I have a new racket."
(6) "It looks terrific. (7) Pam says your game is really improving."

28. Which character says sentence 5?

(a) Matt
b. Emily
c. Pam

29. Which character says sentence 6?

a. Matt
(b) Emily
c. Pam

30. In sentence 6, to what does the word *it* refer?

a. The tennis court
(b) Matt's tennis racket
c. Matt's tennis game

Read the passage below. Then answer items 31–36.

One cold night, I heard some slaves talking about a woman named Moses.

Old George said, "Moses has led so many runaways out of the South that the masters will pay to have her captured—dead or alive."

"She's eight feet tall," Old George continued in a whisper. "She can carry a grown man under each arm and still run faster than any slave catcher."

"That can't be," I said. "I don't believe there is a Moses."

"Yes, there is," Henry said. He was a new slave on the plantation.

"How do you know?" I asked.

"Moses is an old friend of mine," he said. "Her real name is Harriet Tubman. She will come for me

one of these days, and she will take any of you who are brave enough to go."

Moses was real! For the first time in my life, I believed I had a chance to be free. I had been a slave all my life, and I wanted freedom. I had heard stories about how free blacks lived in the north. A free man could own property. He could work for anyone he wanted to, and no one could treat him like an animal.

I wanted to be free, but fear kept me from running away. On the plantation, I had food every day, even if it was never enough. The master gave us clothes to wear and a cabin to sleep in.

How did a free man get food, clothing, and shelter? I did not know, and I was afraid of the unknown world outside the plantation. One thing I did know was that if I ran away and got caught, the master would beat me so hard I might die.

31. Which slaves could go north with Harriet?

a. Any who could pay five thousand dollars
b. Any the masters were willing to set free
(c) Any who were brave enough

32. One sentence says that Harriet is eight feet tall. What type of figurative language does that sentence use?

a. Simile
(b) Exaggeration
c. Metaphor

33. What kept Jim from running away?

(a) Fear of the unknown
b. Fear of animals
c. Fear of running

34. What does Jim not understand about freedom?

a. Why Harriet was called Moses
(b) How free men met their physical needs
c. Why his master would beat him

35. What will Jim probably do next?

a. Go to the master's house for a feast
b. Write a book about being a slave
(c) Think more about Henry's words

---

36. What is the main idea of the passage?

(a) Jim thought about being a free man.
b. Harriet can run faster than the slave catchers.
c. Slaves were treated like animals.

Lessons 81–90

37. In the Harriet Tubman biography, what was Jim's occupation as a free man?

(a) Cabinetmaker
b. Conductor on the Underground Railroad
c. Raiding party leader

38. Why did Jim become a soldier?

a. He would be paid.
(b) He wanted other slaves to be free as he was.
c. His children wanted him to.

39. In *All in Favor*, what does Nancy believe about the vote to join the club?

a. That the vote had to be unanimous
(b) That Sidney, Harriet, and Tom had voted for her
c. That only two votes were needed to join

40. At the end of *All in Favor*, Nancy finds out that her belief was mistaken. What is that an example of?

a. Exaggeration
b. Metaphor
(c) Irony

41. In the 1840s, what problem could electricity in a house have solved?

(a) Heating the house
b. Earning more than a dollar a day
c. Having to walk to school

42. How is a steamboat different from a sailboat?

a. A steamboat doesn't need a captain.
b. A steamboat can travel on a river.
(c) A steamboat has a shallow hull.

43. Here is one main idea from the article about life in the 1840s: *People made wild claims about pills and other medicine.* What is one supporting detail for that main idea?

a. There was no cure for malaria.
(b) One ad said a potion would make you as strong as an Indian chief.
c. Doctors were not allowed to cut up dead people.

44. Here's a fact: *My sister got a part in the play.* Which one of the following items is relevant to the fact?

a. She drove my car to the audition.
b. She says the stage had red curtains.
(c) She has been practicing for weeks.

45. Here is some evidence: *Some of Ashley's skirts are pleated. Ashley wore a skirt today.* So what do you know about Ashley?

a. She wore a pleated skirt today.
(b) She might have worn a pleated skirt today.
c. She didn't wear a pleated skirt today.

46. How did you figure out the answer to item 45?

(a) By making a deduction
b. By combining the sentences
c. By using words from the passage

47. Read these two sentences: *Arizona is the forty-eighth state. Arizona is known as the Grand Canyon State.* What is the correct way to combine the sentences?

a. Arizona, in the Grand Canyon, is the forty-eighth state.
b. Arizona is a state that is the forty-eighth.
(c) Arizona, the forty-eighth state, is known as the Grand Canyon State.

Read the passage below. Then answer items 48–53.

Harriet's last mission during the war was in Virginia, where she worked as a nurse until the Confederacy surrendered in 1865. The war was finally over, and the slaves were free at last. That was worth celebrating.

Harriet had worked as a soldier during the war. She had spied; she had led raiding parties; she had fought in furious battles; she had convinced slaves to leave their plantations; and she had worked as an army nurse. Her great job was completed, but her troubles were not over.

When Harriet returned to Auburn, New York, in 1865, she was treated as a hero. But she had no money. She had never been paid one cent for her efforts during the war, and she was now deep in debt.

A woman named Sarah Bradford helped Harriet earn money. Sarah helped Harriet write a book about her adventures. The book made a fair amount of money, and Sarah gave every cent to Harriet. But the government still refused to pay Harriet for her services.

A lot of people testified that Harriet deserved the money. A general from the North wrote, "She made many a raid inside the enemy lines, displaying remarkable courage." A doctor who worked in a hospital in South Carolina praised her for her "kindness and attention to the sick and suffering." Others told about the unselfish deeds Harriet had done. But the government still refused to pay her.

48. Who kept the money for the book Harriet and Sarah wrote?

a. The government
(b) Harriet
c. The publisher

49. Which one of the following events occurred last?

a. Harriet worked as a nurse.
b. The slaves were freed.
(c) The government refused to pay Harriet.

50. Why did people testify about what Harriet had done during the war?

(a) They wanted the government to pay Harriet for her services.
b. They were writing a book about Harriet.
c. They were trying to help Harriet get a job.

51. Why did Harriet help people during the war?

a. She wanted someone to write a book about her someday.
(b) She was an unselfish person.
c. She wanted to celebrate when the slaves were freed.

52. Where did Harriet live after the war ended?

a. The South
(b) The North
c. Canada

53. How does Harriet probably face her troubles with the government?

a. In a kindly way
b. Laughingly
(c) Courageously

STOP - end of test - SCORE: _____

Recording Individual Results

(Use the following script to record individual results.)

1. Look at your Individual Skills Profile Chart.
2. You're going to record your test results for lesson 90. First look at the test to find out which items you got wrong. Then circle those items on the chart.
3. Now record your results. I'll help you if you have any questions. (Circulate among the students as they record their results.)
4. (After the students finish, say:) Now count the items you did *not* circle and write the total in the **Total** box near the bottom of the column. The total should be the same as your test score.
5. Now you'll fill in the other boxes for lesson 90. If you scored 0 to 42 points, write an **X** in the box marked **Retest.** If you scored 43 to 53 points, write your score in the box marked **FINAL SCORE.**

Remedial Exercises

Students who scored 0 to 42 points on the test should be given remedial help. After the regular reading period is over, assemble these students and present the following exercises. The students will need their original test papers.

EXERCISE 1   Vocabulary Review

1. Let's talk about the meanings of some words.

2. The first term is **quarantine station.** A **quarantine station** is a place where people who may have diseases are kept.
   - Everybody, what's another word for a place where people who may have diseases are kept? (Signal.) *Quarantine station.*

3. The next word is **skiff.** A **skiff** is a small rowboat.
   - Everybody, what's another way of saying **We took a small rowboat up the river**? (Signal.) *We took a skiff up the river.*

4. The next word is **forecastle.** The **forecastle** is a ship's cabin where sailors sleep.
   - Everybody, what's another way of saying **Have you seen the cabin where the sailors sleep?** (Signal.) *Have you seen the forecastle?*

5. The next word is **collide.** When two things **collide,** they run into each other.
   - Everybody, what's another way of saying **We ran into each other in the hall**? (Signal.) *We collided in the hall.*

6. The next word is **churn. Churn** means "to stir up."
   - Everybody, what's another way of saying **The boat is stirring up the water**? (Signal.) *The boat is churning the water.*

7. The next word is **hurtle. Hurtle** means "to move quickly and forcefully."
   - Everybody, what's another way of saying **The car moved quickly and forcefully toward the exit**? (Signal.) *The car hurtled toward the exit.*

8. The next word is **junction.** A **junction** is a place where roads meet.
   - Everybody, what do we call a place where roads meet? (Signal.) *A junction.*

9. The next word is **deception.** When you deceive somebody, you are using **deception** or trickery.
   - Everybody, what do you use when you deceive somebody? (Signal.) *Deception.*

10. The next word is **agony. Agony** means "great pain."
    - Everybody, what's another way of saying **Her broken arm put her in great pain**? (Signal.) *Her broken arm put her in agony.*

11. The next word is **supernatural.** When something is **supernatural,** it seems magical and cannot be explained by science.
    - Everybody, what do we call something that seems magical and can't be explained by science? (Signal.) *Supernatural.*

12. The next word is **plush. Plush** means "fancy and expensive."
    - Everybody, what's another way of saying **Your pink sweater is fancy and expensive**? (Signal.) *Your pink sweater is plush.*

13. The next word is **bulky. Bulky** means "large and heavy."
    - Everybody, what's another of saying **A refrigerator is a large and heavy appliance**? (Signal.) *A refrigerator is a bulky appliance.*

14. The next word is **sensation. Sensation** is another word for **feeling.**
    - Everybody, what's another way of saying **Being on the roller coaster gave me a feeling of dizziness**? (Signal.) *Being on the roller coaster gave me a sensation of dizziness.*

15. The next word is **legend.** A **legend** is an old story about characters who may really have lived.
    - Everybody, what's another way of saying **Do you know any old stories about characters who may really have lived**? (Signal.) *Do you know any legends?*

16. The next word is **exception.** When you make an **exception,** you break the rules for a special case.
    - Everybody, what's another way of saying **Please break the rules for my puppy**? (Signal.) *Please make an exception for my puppy.*

17. The next word is **beforehand. Beforehand** means "before another event."
    - Everybody, what's another way of saying **Were you there before the game**? (Signal.) *Were you there beforehand?*

18. The next word is **systematically.** When something is done **systematically,** it is done in an organized way.
    - Everybody, what's another way of saying **He does his work in an organized way**? (Signal.) *He does his work systematically.*

19. The next word is **dryly.** When you speak **dryly,** you speak without enthusiasm.
    - Everybody, what's another way of saying **She said her lines without enthusiasm**? (Signal.) *She said her lines dryly.*

20. The next word is **defy. Defy** is another word for **challenge** or **oppose.**
    - Everybody, what's another way of saying **My brother challenges the babysitter**? (Signal.) *My brother defies the babysitter.*

21. The next word is **smirk.** When you **smirk,** you give a mocking smile.
    - Everybody, what's another way of saying **Don't give a mocking smile if you win**? (Signal.) *Don't smirk if you win.*

22. The next word is **corridor.** A **corridor** is a hallway.
    - Everybody, what's another way of saying **The school hallways were filled with children**? (Signal.) *The school corridors were filled with children.*

23. The next term is **in debt.** When you are **in debt,** you owe money.
    - Everybody, what's another way of saying **She owes money for lunch**? (Signal.) *She is in debt for lunch.*

24. The next word is **regiment.** A **regiment** is an army unit having a certain number of soldiers.
    - Everybody, what's another way of saying **Which army unit are you in**? (Signal.) *Which regiment are you in?*

25. The last word is **dumbfounded. Dumbfounded** means "briefly astonished."
    - Everybody, what's another way of saying **Raul was briefly astonished when the egg hatched**? (Signal.) *Raul was dumbfounded when the egg hatched.*

EXERCISE 2   General Review

1. I'll name some things that I want to find out. Tell me whether I would find the information in an **atlas,** a **dictionary,** or an **encyclopedia.**
   - The spelling of *unguent* (Response: *Dictionary.*)

- The distance from San Francisco, California, to Miami, Florida (Response: *Atlas.*)
- Who invented the washing machine (Response: *Encyclopedia.*)

2. What type of figurative language uses the word *like*? (Response: *Simile.*)
   - What type of figurative language tells how two things are the same without using the word *like*? (Response: *Metaphor.*)
   - What type of figurative language stretches the truth? (Response: *Exaggeration.*)
   - In what type of figurative language do people say the opposite of what they really mean? (Response: *Sarcasm.*)

3. Everybody, look at the map on page 101 of your test.
   - Two states that border Missouri are labeled. Name those two states. (Response: *Iowa and Arkansas.*)
   - What city is north of St. Louis? (Response: *Minneapolis.*)

4. I'll make some statements about the map. Tell me if each statement is **contradictory** or **not contradictory.**
   - Memphis is north of St. Louis. (Response: *Contradictory.*)
   - Memphis is north of New Orleans. (Response: *Not contradictory.*)

5. When did Jim escape with Harriet? (Idea: *After his master beat him because the horse stumbled and broke its leg.*)
   - After the slaves had walked for several days, how did they travel? (Idea: *By train.*)

6. Who could buy and sell slaves? (Idea: *Masters of plantations.*)
   - Who provided food to slaves? (Idea: *Their masters.*)
   - Who provided food to free men? (Idea: *They had to provide their own food.*)

7. Here's a sentence: *Some people have red hair, but most people don't.*
   - Here's the same sentence with a word missing: *Some people have red hair, but most don't.*
   - What word is missing from that sentence? (Response: *People.*)

8. Everybody, look at the passage at the top of the left column on page 103 of your test. (Call on a student to read the passage aloud.)
   - Which character says sentence 3? (Response: *Emily.*)
   - Which character says sentence 4? (Response: *Matt.*)

9. In sentence 3 of the passage, to whom does *you* refer? (Response: *Matt.*)

10. In the Harriet Tubman biography, who was a cabinetmaker? (Response: *Jim.*)
    - Who conducted slaves to the North? (Response: *Harriet Tubman.*)
    - Who had led raiding parties? (Response: *Harriet Tubman.*)

11. After Jim opened his shop, what did his friends want him to become? (Idea: *A Union soldier.*)
    - What did they remind him of to convince him? (Idea: *His life as a slave.*)

12. In the Harriet Tubman biography, Jim had a mistaken belief about some shelves.
    - At first, why did he believe he was making the shelves? (Idea: *Because Harriet's parents needed them.*)
    - Later, what did he realize was the real reason Harriet asked him to make the shelves? (Idea: *To show that he was capable of working.*)
    - Jim's mistaken belief is an example of something. What is that? (Idea: *Irony.*)

13. Why were the bedrooms cold in the 1840s? (Idea: *There were no electric or gas heaters to warm them.*)

14. What boat has a shallow hull—a steamboat or a sailboat? (Response: *A steamboat.*)

15. What do we call information that helps explain a fact? (Response: *Relevant information.*)
    - What do we call information that does not help explain a fact? (Response: *Irrelevant information.*)

16. Here's a fact: *The girl was running.*
    - Here's some information: *The girl was named Sally.* Is that information relevant or irrelevant to the fact? (**Response:** *Irrelevant.*)
    - Here's some more information: *The girl saw a bear.* Is that information relevant or irrelevant to the fact? (**Response:** *Relevant.*)

17. Here's a sentence that combines two short sentences: *The cottontail, a kind of rabbit, lives in the Southwest.*
    - One short sentence tells where the cottontail lives. Tell me that sentence. (**Response:** *The cottontail lives in the Southwest.*)
    - One short sentence tells what kind of animal the cottontail is. Tell me that sentence. (**Response:** *The cottontail is a kind of rabbit.*)

EXERCISE 3 Passage Reading

Passage 1

1. Everybody, look at the passage on page 102 of your test. You're going to read the passage aloud.

2. (Call on individual students to read several sentences each. Correct any decoding errors. When the students finish, present the following questions.)

3. Who was in the lifeboat first? (**Idea:** *Pete and Frisco Kid.*)
   - Who jumped into the lifeboat next? (**Response:** *Joe.*)

4. Who was trying to get the skiff off the beach? (**Response:** *Bill.*)
   - What was he asking Nick to do? (**Idea:** *Help him.*)
   - What did Nick do instead? (**Idea:** *Tried to get into the lifeboat.*)
   - What happened when he did that? (**Idea:** *He almost sank the lifeboat.*)

5. What were the policemen on the beach doing? (**Idea:** *Shooting at the men.*)

6. What did Frisco Kid tell Nick to do? (**Idea:** *Get out of the boat.*)

7. Who threw Nick out of the boat? (**Idea:** *Frisco Kid and Joe.*)

8. Which boat did Nick get into then? (**Idea:** *The skiff.*)

9. How did the men escape the police? (**Idea:** *By rowing away from the beach.*)

Passage 2

1. Everybody, look at the long passage on page 103 of your test. You're going to read the passage aloud.

2. (Call on individual students to read several sentences each. Correct any decoding errors. When the students finish, present the following questions.)

3. Who did Henry say was coming for him? (**Idea:** *Harriet Tubman.*)
   - What was Harriet's nickname? (**Response:** *Moses.*)

4. How does Old George describe Harriet? (**Ideas:** *She's eight feet tall; she could carry a grown man under each arm and still run faster than the slave catchers.*)

5. How long had Jim been a slave? (**Idea:** *All his life.*)
   - What did he want? (**Idea:** *Freedom.*)

6. What did Jim get every day on the plantation? (**Idea:** *Food.*)

7. How did Jim think free men get food? (**Idea:** *He didn't know.*)

8. What did Jim think the master would do if Jim ran away and was later caught? (**Idea:** *Beat him.*)

Passage 3

1. Everybody, look at the passage on page 105 of your test. You're going to read the passage aloud.

2. (Call on individual students to read several sentences each. Correct any decoding errors. When the students finish, present the following questions.)

3. Who wrote a book about Harriet's adventures? (Idea: *Sarah Bradford and Harriet.*)
   • What did Sarah Bradford do with the money earned from the book? (Idea: *She gave it to Harriet.*)

4. Did the book sell well? (Response: *Yes.*)

5. When was Harriet a nurse? (Idea: *During the Civil War.*)
   • Were the slaves free after the war? (Response: *Yes.*)

6. When the government wouldn't pay Harriet, what did many people do? (Idea: *Testified about the courageous and unselfish deeds Harriet had done.*)

7. Is New York located in the North or in the South? (Response: *In the North.*)

8. Name one dangerous deed Harriet had done. (Idea: *She conducted a raid inside enemy lines.*)
   • What kind of trait did this show? (Idea: *Courage.*)

Retesting the Students

After you've completed the remedial exercises, retest each student individually. To administer the retest, you will need the student's original test paper, a blank copy of the test, and a red pencil. Give the student the blank copy of the test. Say, "Look at page 100. You're going to take this test again. Read each item aloud and tell me the answer."

Use the student's original test paper to grade the retest. Use the red pencil to mark each correct answer with a **C** and each incorrect answer with an **X**. Then count one point for each correct answer and write the new score at the bottom of the page. Finally, revise the Individual Skills Profile Chart by drawing an **X** over any items the student missed on the retest.

Complete the Group Point Chart for lesson 90.

Administering the Checkouts

You can conduct checkouts by using the passage on page 105 of the Lesson 90 Mastery Test. See page 9 for a complete description of checkout procedures.

Tested Skills and Concepts

The Lesson 90 Mastery Test measures student mastery of the following skills and concepts.

- using vocabulary words in context (items 1–6)
- using context to predict word meaning (items 7–12)
- identifying proper reference sources (item 13)
- interpreting figurative language (items 14–16 and 32)
- interpreting maps (items 17 and 18)
- identifying contradictions (item 19)
- answering literal questions about a text (items 20, 31, and 48)
- inferring story details and events (item 21)
- distinguishing characters by trait (item 22)
- drawing conclusions (item 23)
- interpreting substitute words (items 24 and 30)
- sequencing narrative events (items 25 and 49)
- making comparisons (items 26 and 42)
- interpreting shortened sentences (item 27)
- interpreting extended dialogues (items 28 and 29)
- inferring causes and effects (items 33 and 38)
- inferring a character's point of view (item 34)
- predicting a character's actions (item 35)
- inferring the main idea (item 36)
- recalling details and events (items 37 and 39)
- interpreting irony (item 40)
- evaluating problems and solutions (item 41)
- inferring details relevant to a main idea (item 43)
- identifying relevant evidence (item 44)
- completing written deductions (item 45)
- identifying inferential questions (item 46)
- interpreting combined sentences (item 47)
- identifying literal cause and effect (item 50)
- interpreting a character's motives (item 51)
- distinguishing settings by features (item 52)
- interpreting a character's feelings (item 53)

Lesson 100

Administering the Test

The Lesson 100 Mastery Test should be administered after the students complete all work on lesson 100 and before they begin work on lesson 101. Each student will need a pencil and a copy of the test. Use the following script.

1. (Have the students clear their desks. Make sure each student has a pencil.)
2. Now you're going to take another test on what you've learned. I'll give each of you a copy of the test. Don't begin until I tell you. (Pass out the tests.)
3. Write your name on the name line in the upper right-hand corner of each page.
4. Now you're ready to begin the test. Answer all the items on each page. There is no time limit. When you've finished, turn your test facedown and look up at me. Begin the test now. (If you are including the writing item as part of the testing session, tell students they can begin the writing item after they finish the mastery test.)

Grading the Test

You can grade the tests yourself, or you can have the students grade one another's tests. If you want the students to grade one another's tests, tell them to trade test papers. Then use the following script.

1. Now we're going to grade the test. I'll read the correct answer for each item. If the answer is correct, mark it with a **C**. If the answer is wrong, mark it with an **X**.
2. (Read the correct answers from the answer key on this page and the next.)
3. Now count the number of **correct** answers and enter the score at the end of the test.

Answer Key

Lesson 100

Name _____

For items 1–8, circle the letter of the answer that means the same thing as the underlined part.

1. The boy was so underlined deeply involved in his reading that he didn't hear the phone ring.
   a. harassed
   b. casual
   c. absorbed

2. The girl made a underlined mistake on her test.
   a. scuffle
   b. sermon
   c. blunder

3. I was underlined puzzled by her strange remark.
   a. perplexed
   b. considerable
   c. foolhardy

4. She slept underlined lightly on the train trip.
   a. lulled
   b. dozed
   c. sidled

5. The jeweler looked closely at the diamond to see if it was underlined genuine.
   a. real
   b. large
   c. red

6. The astronomer underlined contemplated the vastness of space.
   a. ignored
   b. was afraid of
   c. thought about

7. The president repeated the underlined oath of office as he was sworn in.
   a. solemn promise
   b. essay
   c. application

8. We walked underlined gingerly on the icy street.
   a. hurriedly
   b. cautiously
   c. backward

For items 9–23, circle the letter of the correct answer.

9. Here is some evidence: *Some of my cousins live in Texas. Mike is my cousin. So what do you know about Mike?*
   a. Maybe he lives in Texas.
   b. He lives in Texas.
   c. He doesn't live in Texas.

10. In the following sentence, the star shows where a word is missing. *Five * were ill, but the other members came to the meeting at the field.*
    a. meetings
    b. members
    c. fields

11. Here's a sentence that combines two short sentences. *Tom painted the fence with whitewash, a watery white substance.* The first short sentence is *Tom painted the fence with whitewash.* What is the second short sentence?
    a. Whitewash is a watery white substance.
    b. That paint is whitewash.
    c. That paint is a white, watery substance.

12. If you want to know how to pronounce the word *cough*, which reference book would you use?
    a. Atlas
    b. Encyclopedia
    c. Dictionary

106   Reading Mastery Plus, Level 6

Name _____

13. What problems did Aunt Polly have in disciplining Tom?
    a. He was bigger than she was.
    b. He would always run into the church.
    c. She didn't have the heart to punish him.

14. Where did Outlaw Joe kill Dr. Robinson?
    a. In the graveyard
    b. In the schoolyard
    c. Behind Tom's fence

In the paragraph below, the sentences are numbered. Read the paragraph. Then answer items 15 and 16.

(1) Ben was talking to Tom as Tom was white-washing the fence. (2) "But of course you'd rather work than go swimming, wouldn't you?" said Ben. (3) When Tom ignored him, Ben said, "Oh, come on, let me whitewash a little bit. I'll be careful."

15. Which statement is a sample of sarcasm?
    a. 1
    b. 2
    c. 3

16. Which statement contradicts the sarcastic statement?
    a. 1
    b. 2
    c. 3

17. How did students do their writing assignments in the 1840s?
    a. With slates and chalk
    b. With their fingers in the air
    c. On typewriters

Read the passage below. Then answer items 18–23.

When Tom reached the little frame schoolhouse that Monday morning, he walked in briskly. He hung his hat on a peg and flung himself into his seat. The schoolmaster was dozing in front of the class in his great wooden armchair. He had been lulled to sleep by the drowsy hum of study. Tom's entrance woke him.

"Thomas Sawyer!"

Tom knew that when his name was pronounced in full, it meant trouble.

"Sir!"

"Come up here. Why are you late again, as usual?"

Tom was about to lie when he saw two long tails of yellow hair hanging down a back that he recognized. It was the Adored Unknown Girl! And next to her was the only vacant place on the girls' side of the schoolhouse.

Tom instantly said, "I STOPPED TO TALK WITH HUCKLEBERRY FINN!"

The schoolmaster's heart stopped, and he stared helplessly. The buzz of study ceased. The pupils wondered if this foolhardy boy had lost his mind. The master said:

"You . . . did what?"

"Stopped to talk with Huckleberry Finn."

There was no mistaking the words.

"Thomas Sawyer, this is the most astounding confession I have ever listened to. You will be punished for this."

Then the order followed: "Thomas Sawyer, I order you to go and sit with the girls! And let this be a warning to you."

18. Why was Tom late for school?
    a. He stopped to talk with Huck Finn.
    b. He was lulled to sleep by the hum of study.
    c. He had forgotten his books.

19. Why did Tom tell the schoolmaster the truth?
    a. He was afraid of the schoolmaster.
    b. He wanted to sit with the girls.
    c. He was not a good liar.

Lesson 100 Test   107

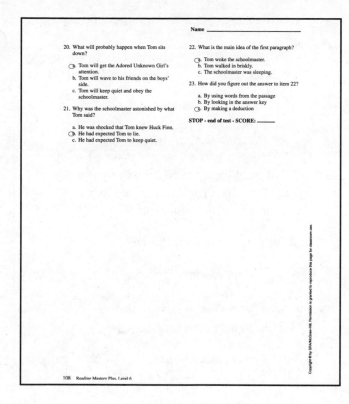

Name _____

20. What will probably happen when Tom sits down?

   a. Tom will get the Adored Unknown Girl's attention.
   b. Tom will wave to his friends on the boys' side.
   c. Tom will keep quiet and obey the schoolmaster.

21. Why was the schoolmaster astonished by what Tom said?

   a. He was shocked that Tom knew Huck Finn.
   b. He had expected Tom to lie.
   c. He had expected Tom to keep quiet.

22. What is the main idea of the first paragraph?

   a. Tom woke the schoolmaster.
   b. Tom walked in briskly.
   c. The schoolmaster was sleeping.

23. How did you figure out the answer to item 22?

   a. By using words from the passage
   b. By looking in the answer key
   c. By making a deduction

STOP - end of test - SCORE: _____

108   Reading Mastery Plus, Level 6

Recording Individual Results

(Use the following script to record individual results.)

1. Look at your Individual Skills Profile Chart.
2. You're going to record your test results for lesson 100. First look at the test to find out which items you got wrong. Then circle those items on the chart.
3. Now record your results. I'll help you if you have any questions. **(Circulate among the students as they record their results.)**
4. **(After the students finish, say:)** Now count the items you did *not* circle and write the total in the **Total** box near the bottom of the column. The total should be the same as your test score.
5. Now you'll fill in the other boxes for lesson 100. If you scored 0 to 18 points, write an **X** in the box marked **Retest.** If you scored 19 to 23 points, write your score in the box marked **FINAL SCORE.**

Remedial Exercises

Students who scored 0 to 18 points on the test should be given remedial help. After the regular reading period is over, assemble these students and present the following exercises. The students will need their original test papers.

EXERCISE 1   Vocabulary Review

1. Let's talk about the meanings of some words.

2. The first word is **harass.** When you **harass** somebody, you taunt or tease that person.
   • Everybody, what's another way of saying **She taunted and teased her brother**? (Signal.) *She harassed her brother.*

3. The next word is **casual.** When something is **casual,** it happens by chance or at random.
   • Everybody, what's another way of saying **The cousins had a chance meeting**? (Signal.) *The cousins had a casual meeting.*

4. The next word is **absorbed.** When you are **absorbed** in something, you are deeply involved in it.
   • Everybody, what's another way of saying **The woman was deeply involved in her work**? (Signal.) *The woman was absorbed in her work.*

5. The next word is **scuffle.** A **scuffle** is a small fight.
   • Everybody, what's another way of saying **The cats got into a small fight**? (Signal.) *The cats got into a scuffle.*

6. The next word is **sermon.** A **sermon** is a speech that a minister delivers in church.
   • Everybody, what's another way of saying **The minister's speech was about forgiveness**? (Signal.) *The sermon was about forgiveness.*

7. The next word is **blunder.** A **blunder** is a mistake.
   • Everybody, what's another way of saying **The student made a mistake on the test**? (Signal.) *The student made a blunder on the test.*

8. The next word is **perplexed. Perplexed** is another word for **puzzled.**
   • Everybody, what's another way of saying **He was puzzled about the theft**? (Signal.) *He was perplexed about the theft.*

9. The next word is **considerable.** Something that is **considerable** is large or great.
   • Everybody, what's another way of saying **Bennett took a large amount of salad**? (Signal.) *Bennett took a considerable amount of salad.*

10. The next word is **foolhardy.** When you are foolishly bold, you are **foolhardy.**
    • Everybody, what's another way of saying **It was foolishly bold to carry that box**? (Signal.) *It was foolhardy to carry that box.*

11. The next word is **lulled.** When something **lulls** you, it makes you sleepy or relaxed.
    • Everybody, what's another way of saying **The soft music made him sleepy**? (Signal.) *The soft music lulled him.*

12. The next word is **dozed.** Someone who is **dozing** is sleeping lightly.
    • Everybody, what's another way of saying **Can you sleep lightly on the sofa?** (Signal.) *Can you doze on the sofa?*

13. The next word is **sidled.** When you **sidle,** you move sideways.
    • Everybody, what's another way of saying **The child moved sideways toward his father**? (Signal.) *The child sidled toward his father.*

14. The next word is **genuine.** Something that is **genuine** is real.
    • Everybody, what's another way of saying **The necklace was made of real pearls**? (Signal.) *The necklace was made of genuine pearls.*

15. The next word is **contemplate.** When you **contemplate** something, you think about it.
    • Everybody, what's another way of saying **The chess player thought about his next move**? (Signal.) *The chess player contemplated his next move*.

16. The next word is **oath.** An **oath** is a solemn promise.
    • Everybody, what's another way of saying **A solemn promise is important**? (Signal.) *An oath is important.*

17. The last word is **gingerly. Gingerly** is another word for **cautiously.**
    • Everybody, what's another way of saying **The zookeeper approached the snake cautiously**? (Signal.) *The zookeeper approached the snake gingerly.*

EXERCISE 2   General Review

1. Here is some evidence: *Some cakes are round. John has a cake.*
   • So what do you know about John's cake? (Idea: *It may be round.*)

2. Here's a sentence: *Nancy was in class, but Julie wasn't in class.*
   Here's the same sentence with some words missing: *Nancy was in class, but Julie wasn't.*
   • What words are missing from the sentence? (Response: *In class.*)

3. Here's a sentence that combines two short sentences: *The dingo, a kind of dog, lives in Australia.*
   • One short sentence tells where the dog lives. Tell me that sentence. (Response: *The dingo lives in Australia.*)
   • One short sentence tells what kind of animal the dingo is. Tell me that sentence. (Response: *The dingo is a kind of dog.*)

4. I'll name some things I want to find out. Tell me whether I would find the information in an **atlas,** a **dictionary,** or an **encyclopedia.**
   • The spelling of *magnanimous* (Response: *Dictionary.*)
   • What countries border Austria (Ideas: *Atlas; encyclopedia.*)
   • Who discovered Pluto (Response: *Encyclopedia.*)

5. Why did Tom live with Aunt Polly? (Idea: *His mother, Polly's sister, had died.*)
   • Every time Aunt Polly punished Tom, how did she feel? (Idea: *It made her heart almost break.*)

6. Where did Tom and Huck go one night? (Idea: *To the graveyard*.)
   - What did they see there? (Ideas: *Dr. Robinson, Muff Potter, and Outlaw Joe were digging and got into an argument; Outlaw Joe killed the doctor but blamed it on Potter*.)

7. Sometimes, people say the opposite of what they really mean. What is the word for that type of figurative language? (Response: *Sarcasm*.)

8. What were schools like in the 1840s? (Ideas: *Some schoolrooms held students of all ages, with boys on one side of the room and girls on the other side; the students sat on long benches*.)
   - How did the students do their schoolwork? (Ideas: *They read aloud; they wrote with chalk on slates*.)

EXERCISE 3   Passage Reading

1. Everybody, look at the passage on page 107 of your test. You're going to read the passage aloud.

2. (Call on individual students to read several sentences each. Correct any decoding errors. When the students finish, present the following questions.)

3. With whom had Tom stopped to talk? (Response: *Huckleberry Finn*.)

4. Whom did Tom want to sit beside? (Idea: *The Adored Unknown Girl*.)
   - Tom knew that the schoolmaster would do something to punish him. What was that? (Idea: *Make him sit with the girls*.)
   - So did Tom lie to the schoolmaster or tell him the truth? (Idea: *Told him the truth*.)

5. Did the schoolmaster expect Tom to lie? (Response: *Yes*.)
   - How did he feel when Tom told the truth? (Ideas: *Surprised; astonished*.)

6. What do you think Tom will do while he sits beside the Adored Unknown Girl? (Ideas: *Talk to her; try to get her attention*.)

7. I'll read a paragraph from the passage: "The schoolmaster's heart stopped, and he stared helplessly. The buzz of study ceased. The pupils wondered if this foolhardy boy had lost his mind."
   - The paragraph mentions several people who feel the same way. How do those people feel? (Ideas: *Astonished; amazed*.)
   - So what's the main idea of the paragraph? (Ideas: *Everyone was astonished; everyone was amazed*.)

Retesting the Students

After you've completed the remedial exercises, retest each student individually. To administer the retest, you will need the student's original test paper, a blank copy of the test, and a red pencil. Give the student the blank copy of the test. Say, "Look at page 106. You're going to take this test again. Read each item aloud and tell me the answer."

Use the student's original test paper to grade the retest. Use the red pencil to mark each correct answer with a **C** and each incorrect answer with an **X**. Then count one point for each correct answer and write the new score at the bottom of the page. Finally, revise the Individual Skills Profile Chart by drawing an **X** over any items the student missed on the retest.

Complete the Group Point Chart for lesson 100.

Administering the Checkouts

You can conduct checkouts by using the passage on page 107 of the Lesson 100 Mastery Test. See page 9 for a complete description of checkout procedures.

Tested Skills and Concepts

The Lesson 100 Mastery Test measures student mastery of the following skills and concepts.

- using vocabulary words in context (items 1–4)
- using context to predict word meaning (items 5–8)
- completing written deductions (item 9)
- interpreting shortened sentences (item 10)
- interpreting combined sentences (item 11)
- identifying proper reference sources (item 12)
- evaluating problems and solutions (item 13)
- distinguishing settings by features (item 14)
- interpreting figurative language (item 15)
- identifying contradictions (item 16)
- recalling details and events (item 17)
- identifying literal cause and effect (item 18)
- inferring causes and effects (item 19)
- predicting narrative outcomes (item 20)
- inferring a character's point of view (item 21)
- inferring the main idea (item 22)
- identifying inferential questions (item 23)

Lesson 110

Administering the Test

The Lesson 110 Mastery Test should be administered after the students complete all work on lesson 110 and before they begin work on lesson 111. Each student will need a pencil and a copy of the test. Use the following script.

1. (Have the students clear their desks. Make sure each student has a pencil.)
2. Now you're going to take another test on what you've learned. I'll give each of you a copy of the test. Don't begin until I tell you. (Pass out the tests.)
3. Write your name on the name line in the upper right-hand corner of each page.
4. Now you're ready to begin the test. Answer all the items on each page. There is no time limit. When you've finished, turn your test facedown and look up at me. Begin the test now. (If you are including the writing item as part of the testing session, tell students they can begin the writing item after they finish the mastery test.)

Grading the Test

You can grade the tests yourself, or you can have the students grade one another's tests. If you want the students to grade one another's tests, tell them to trade test papers. Then use the following script.

1. Now we're going to grade the test. I'll read the correct answer for each item. If the answer is correct, mark it with a C. If the answer is wrong, mark it with an X.
2. (Read the correct answers from the answer key on this page and the next.)
3. Now count the number of correct answers and enter the score at the end of the test.

Answer Key

Lesson 110

Name _____

For items 1–8, circle the letter of the answer that means the same thing as the underlined part.

1. Everyone was shocked by the horrible accident.
   a. haggard
   b. blissful
   c. ghastly

2. The hamlet was completely destroyed by the violent storm.
   a. utterly
   b. confidentially
   c. randomly

3. Was there a great high point at the end of the story?
   a. topic
   b. climax
   c. folly

4. He dug up the toy from the pile of laundry.
   a. unearthed
   b. abused
   c. chartered

5. The old woman reflected on the events of her life.
   a. looked at
   b. rejected
   c. thought about

6. My brother played hooky once.
   a. didn't go to school
   b. was on the hooky team
   c. shot a bow and arrow

7. Eduardo seemed jealous when Paula received the prize he wanted.
   a. embarrassed
   b. happy
   c. suspicious

8. An X on the map made the location of the treasure distinct.
   a. easy to recognize
   b. hard to see
   c. uncertain

For items 9–24, circle the letter of the correct answer.

9. What was the gift Tom had given Becky?
   a. A piece of blue bottle glass
   b. A dead rat
   c. A brass doorknob

10. Why did Tom talk about the murder in his sleep?
    a. He was trying to scare Sid.
    b. He was dreaming about the murder.
    c. He wanted Aunt Polly to know he had seen the murder.

11. In the following sentence, the star shows where a word is missing. Two * did not join in, but the other students had a good time riding the horses and petting the sheep. What word is missing?
    a. horses
    b. sheep
    c. students

Lesson 110 Test   109

Name _____

12. Here are two sentences: *William Wordsworth wrote about the beauty of nature. William Wordsworth was an important British poet.* Which is a correct way to combine those two sentences?
    a. William Wordsworth wrote about the beauty of nature, an important British poet.
    b. William Wordsworth wrote about important British poets.
    c. William Wordsworth, an important British poet, wrote about the beauty of nature.

13. Here's an argument: *My motorcycle has Haltem brakes, which are the best brakes money can buy. Because the brakes are so good, I'm certain that my motorcycle is the best around.* Which rule does the argument break?
    a. Just because you know about the whole thing doesn't mean you know about every part.
    b. Just because you know about one part doesn't mean you know about another part.
    c. Just because you know about a part doesn't mean you know about the whole thing.

14. Here's an argument: *That factory produces a lot of smoke, and the smoke makes people sick. If we don't close down that factory, everybody will get sick.* Which rule does the argument break?
    a. Just because two things happen around the same time doesn't mean that one thing causes the other thing.
    b. Just because two words sound the same doesn't mean they have the same meaning.
    c. Just because the writer presents some choices doesn't mean that there are no other choices.

Read the facts and instructions below. Then answer items 15 and 16.

Facts:
Your full name is Edna Ferber Millay. You live at 727 Lake Street in Boomwater, North Dakota. You have three children whose names are Craig, Linda, and Derek.
Instructions:
• On line 1, write your full name, but name first.
• On line 2, write the name of the state you live in.

15. What will you write on line 1?
    a. Millay, Edna
    b. Millay, Edna Ferber
    c. Edna Ferber Millay

16. What will you write on line 2?
    a. Boomwater
    b. Dakota
    c. North Dakota

110   Reading Mastery Plus, Level 6

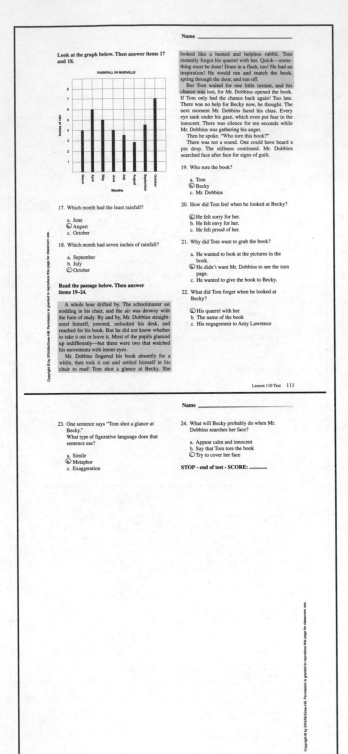

Name _____

Look at the graph below. Then answer items 17 and 18.

RAINFALL IN MUDVILLE

17. Which month had the least rainfall?

   a. June
   ⓑ August
   c. October

18. Which month had seven inches of rainfall?

   a. September
   b. July
   ⓒ October

Read the passage below. Then answer items 19–24.

A whole hour drifted by. The schoolmaster sat nodding in his chair, and the air was drowsy with the hum of study. By and by, Mr. Dobbins straightened himself, yawned, unlocked his desk, and reached for his book. But he did not know whether to take it out or leave it. Most of the pupils glanced up indifferently—but there were two that watched his movements with intent eyes. Mr. Dobbins fingered his book absently for a while, then took it out and settled himself in his chair to read! Tom shot a glance at Becky. She

looked like a hunted and helpless rabbit. Tom instantly forgot his quarrel with her. Quick—something must be done! Done in a flash, too! He had an inspiration! He would run and snatch the book, spring through the door, and run off.

But Tom waited for one little instant, and his chance was lost, for Mr. Dobbins opened the book. If Tom only had the chance back again! Too late. There was no help for Becky now, he thought. The next moment Mr. Dobbins faced his class. Every eye sank under his gaze, which even put fear in the innocent. There was silence for ten seconds while Mr. Dobbins was gathering his anger.

Then he spoke. "Who tore this book?"

There was not a sound. One could have heard a pin drop. The stillness continued. Mr. Dobbins searched face after face for signs of guilt.

19. Who tore the book?

   a. Tom
   ⓑ Becky
   c. Mr. Dobbins

20. How did Tom feel when he looked at Becky?

   ⓐ He felt sorry for her.
   b. He felt envy for her.
   c. He felt proud of her.

21. Why did Tom want to grab the book?

   a. He wanted to look at the pictures in the book.
   ⓑ He didn't want Mr. Dobbins to see the torn page.
   c. He wanted to give the book to Becky.

22. What did Tom forget when he looked at Becky?

   ⓐ His quarrel with her
   b. The name of the book
   c. His engagement to Amy Lawrence

Name _____

23. One sentence says "Tom shot a glance at Becky."
What type of figurative language does that sentence use?

   a. Simile
   ⓑ Metaphor
   c. Exaggeration

24. What will Becky probably do when Mr. Dobbins searches her face?

   a. Appear calm and innocent
   b. Say that Tom tore the book
   ⓒ Try to cover her face

STOP - end of test - SCORE: _____

Recording Individual Results

(Use the following script to record individual results.)

1. Look at your Individual Skills Profile Chart.
2. You're going to record your test results for lesson 110. First look at the test to find out which items you got wrong. Then circle those items on the chart.
3. Now record your results. I'll help you if you have any questions. (Circulate among the students as they record their results.)
4. (After the students finish, say:) Now count the items you did *not* circle and write the total in the **Total** box near the bottom of the column. The total should be the same as your test score.
5. Now you'll fill in the other boxes for lesson 110. If you scored 0 to 19 points, write an **X** in the box marked **Retest.** If you scored 20 to 24 points, write your score in the box marked **FINAL SCORE.**

Remedial Exercises

Students who scored 0 to 19 points on the test should be given remedial help. After the regular reading period is over, assemble these students and present the following exercises. The students will need their original test papers.

EXERCISE 1   Vocabulary Review

1. Let's talk about the meanings of some words.

2. The first word is **haggard.** When someone is very tired, that person looks **haggard.**
   • Everybody, what's another way of saying **The old man looked very tired**? (Signal.) *The old man looked haggard.*

3. The next word is **blissful. Blissful** is another word for **joyful.**
   • Everybody, what's another way of saying **A wedding is a joyful event**? (Signal.) *A wedding is a blissful event.*

4. The next word is **ghastly.** Something that is horrible is **ghastly.**
   - Everybody, what's another way of saying **The monster let out a horrible scream**? (Signal.) *The monster let out a ghastly scream.*

5. The next word is **utterly. Utterly** is another word for **completely.**
   - Everybody, what's another way of saying **The army was completely defeated**? (Signal.) *The army was utterly defeated.*

6. The next word is **confidential.** When something is **confidential,** it is private or secret.
   - Everybody, what's another way of saying **This letter is private**? (Signal.) *This letter is confidential.*

7. The next word is **randomly.** If something is done without any pattern, that thing is done **randomly.**
   - Everybody, what's another way of saying **She walked around without any pattern**? (Signal.) *She walked around randomly.*

8. The next word is **topic. Topic** is another word for **subject.**
   - Everybody, what's another way of saying **What is the subject of your composition?** (Signal.) *What is the topic of your composition?*

9. The next word is **climax.** The **climax** of a story is the story's most important event or highest point.
   - Everybody, what's another way of saying **We had to leave before the movie's highest point**? (Signal.) *We had to leave before the movie's climax.*

10. The next word is **folly. Folly** is a foolish act.
    - Everybody, what's another way of saying **Skating without a helmet is a foolish act**? (Signal.) *Skating without a helmet is folly.*

11. The next word is **unearth.** When you **unearth** something, you dig it up.
    - Everybody, what's another way of saying **The squirrel is digging up the nut it hid last fall**? (Signal.) *The squirrel is unearthing the nut it hid last fall.*

12. The next word is **abuse.** When you **abuse** something, you treat it badly.
    - Everybody, what's another way of saying **He treated his little brother badly**? (Signal.) *He abused his little brother.*

13. The next word is **charter.** When you **charter** a vehicle, you rent the vehicle for a group of people.
    - Everybody, what's another way of saying **The senior club rented a van for the trip**? (Signal.) *The senior club chartered a van for the trip.*

14. The next word is **reflect.** When you **reflect** on something, you ponder that thing.
    - Everybody, what's another way of saying **The woman pondered her accomplishments**? (Signal.) *The woman reflected on her accomplishments.*

15. The next term is **play hooky.** When you **play hooky,** you don't go to school when you are supposed to.
    - Everybody, what's another way of saying **Did you not go to school when you were supposed to on Friday**? (Signal.) *Did you play hooky on Friday?*

16. The next word is **jealous.** When you are **jealous,** you are suspicious of other people.
    - Everybody, what's another way of saying **She was suspicious when her friend got a new bike**? (Signal.) *She was jealous when her friend got a new bike.*

17. The last word is **distinct. Distinct** means "easy to recognize."
    - Everybody, what's another way of saying **The faces in the old photograph were not easy to recognize**? (Signal.) *The faces in the old photograph were not distinct.*

EXERCISE 2   General Review

1. What are some of the items Tom received from his friends for letting them whitewash the fence? (Ideas: *A piece of blue bottle glass; a spool of thread; a tin soldier; tadpoles; firecrackers; a brass doorknob; a dog collar.*)

2. How did Tom's secret affect his sleep? (Idea: *His sleep was disturbed.*)
   - What did he say in his sleep? (Idea: *"It's blood, it's blood. Don't torment me—I'll tell."*)
   - What did he do at night after that so he wouldn't talk? (Idea: *He tied up his jaws.*)

3. Here's a sentence: *Some people left, but most people stayed.*
   - Here's the same sentence with a word missing: *Some people left, but most stayed.*
   - What word is missing from that sentence? (Response: *People.*)

4. Here's a sentence that combines two short sentences: *Charles Ives, an American composer, wrote four symphonies.*
   - One short sentence tells how many symphonies Charles Ives wrote. Tell me that sentence. (Response: *Charles Ives wrote four symphonies.*)
   - One short sentence tells what kind of composer Charles Ives was. Tell me that sentence. (Response: *Charles Ives was an American composer.*)

5. Here's another rule: *Just because you know about the whole thing doesn't mean you know about every part.*
   - Here's an argument that breaks the rule: *Harwood College is one of the best schools in the country. John Doe goes to Harwood College. Therefore, John Doe must be one of the best students in the country.*
   - Which thing in the argument is the whole thing? (Response: *Harwood College.*)
   - Which thing is the part? (Response: *John Doe.*)
   - What conclusion does the writer draw about John Doe? (Idea: *That he must be one of the best students in the country.*)

6. Here's another rule: *Just because the writer presents some choices doesn't mean that there are no other choices.*
   - Here's an argument that breaks the rule: *My neighbor owns a dog. I'm afraid of dogs. If I don't buy a dog, I'll always be afraid.*
   - Which choice does the writer present? (Idea: *Buying a dog.*)
   - Name some other choices the writer could make. (Ideas: *Asking the neighbor to keep the dog chained; learning to overcome fear of dogs; moving away.*)

7. Everybody, look at the graph on page 111 of your test.
   - Which month had the most rainfall? (Response: *October.*)
   - Which month had less than three inches of rainfall? (Response: *August.*)

EXERCISE 3   Passage Reading

1. Everybody, look at the passage on page 111 of your test. You're going to read the passage aloud.

2. (Call on individual students to read several sentences each. Correct any decoding errors. When the students finish, present the following questions.)

3. Which character looked guilty? (Response: *Becky.*)
   - Will it be easy for Becky to change her expression? (Idea: *Probably not.*)

4. When did Tom begin to feel sorry for Becky? (Idea: *When he looked at her.*)

5. How could Tom have prevented Mr. Dobbins from seeing the book? (Idea: *By running up and grabbing it.*)

6. Here's a sentence: *Amy chirped on and on.*
   - What is Amy being compared to? (Idea: *A bird.*)
   - So what kind of figurative language does that sentence use? (Response: *Metaphor.*)

Retesting the Students

After you've completed the remedial exercises, retest each student individually. To administer the retest, you will need the student's original test paper, a blank copy of the test, and a red pencil. Give the student the blank copy of the test. Say, "Look at page 109. You're going to take this test again. Read each item aloud and tell me the answer."

Use the student's original test paper to grade the retest. Use the red pencil to mark each correct answer with a **C** and each incorrect answer with an **X**. Then count one point for each correct answer and write the new score at the bottom of the page. Finally, revise the Individual Skills Profile Chart by drawing an **X** over any items the student missed on the retest.

Complete the Group Point Chart for lesson 110.

Administering the Checkouts

You can conduct checkouts by using the passage on page 111 of the Lesson 110 Mastery Test. See page 9 for a complete description of checkout procedures.

Tested Skills and Concepts

The Lesson 110 Mastery Test measures student mastery of the following skills and concepts.

- using vocabulary words in context (items 1–4)
- using context to predict word meaning (items 5–8)
- recalling details and events (item 9)
- drawing conclusions (item 10)
- interpreting shortened sentences (item 11)
- interpreting combined sentences (item 12)
- identifying logical fallacies (items 13 and 14)
- filling out forms (items 15 and 16)
- interpreting graphs (items 17 and 18)
- inferring story details and events (item 19)
- interpreting a character's feelings (item 20)
- interpreting a character's motives (item 21)
- answering literal questions about a text (item 22)
- interpreting figurative language (item 23)
- predicting a character's actions (item 24)

Lesson 120

Administering the Test

The Lesson 120 Mastery Test should be administered after the students complete all work on lesson 120. Each student will need a pencil and a copy of the test. Use the following script.

1. (Have the students clear their desks. Make sure each student has a pencil.)
2. Now you're going to take another test on what you've learned. This test will be longer than the others you've taken because it has questions about the last thirty lessons. I'll give each of you a copy of the test. Don't begin until I tell you. (Pass out the tests.)
3. Write your name on the name line in the upper right-hand corner of each page.
4. Now you're ready to begin the test. Answer all the items on each page. There is no time limit. When you've finished, turn your test facedown and look up at me. Begin the test now. (If you are including the writing item as part of the testing session, tell students they can begin the writing item after they finish the mastery test.)

Grading the Test

You can grade the tests yourself, or you can have the students grade one another's tests. If you want the students to grade one another's tests, tell them to trade test papers. Then use the following script.

1. Now we're going to grade the test. I'll read the correct answer for each item. If the answer is correct, mark it with a **C.** If the answer is wrong, mark it with an **X.**
2. (Read the correct answers from the answer key on this page and the next.)
3. Now count the number of **correct** answers and enter the score at the end of the test.

Answer Key

Lesson 120

Name _____

For items 1–12, circle the letter of the answer that means the same thing as the underlined part.

1. The movie was about a violent train robber in the Old West.
   a. mortified
   b. vicious
   c. tranquil

2. The team was humiliated after being beaten by fifty points.
   a. crestfallen
   b. indifferent
   c. immortal

3. After many years, the dog began to look like its master.
   a. revive
   b. resemble
   c. elude

4. It was difficult climbing the steep cliff by the river.
   a. loft
   b. inlet
   c. bluff

5. The thief was a liar and a mean person.
   a. deputy
   b. sentry
   c. scoundrel

6. The visit to the war museum had a powerful effect on the students.
   a. impact
   b. relic
   c. catastrophe

7. I'd like a book for a juvenile who is fourteen.
   a. young person
   b. nonfiction
   c. reference

8. The difficult directions flustered him.
   a. confused
   b. angered
   c. worried

9. She hit her head on a stalactite.
   a. rock that forms on the floor of a cave
   b. rock that hangs from the ceiling of a cave
   c. metal supporting rod drilled into the wall of a cave

10. When I saw the hamburger, I realized how famished I was.
    a. hungry
    b. ill
    c. happy

11. The hamlet had only ten houses.
    a. short street
    b. small village
    c. road along the seacoast

12. The camp furnishes all craft materials.
    a. supplies
    b. discards
    c. chooses

For items 13–49, circle the letter of the correct answer.

Lessons 91–100

13. Who was raising Tom Sawyer?
    a. Outlaw Joe
    b. Huckleberry Finn
    c. Aunt Polly

Lesson 120 Test   113

Name _____

14. What did Huck Finn say dead rats could be used for?
    a. To cure warts
    b. To attract a girl
    c. To ward off evil spirits

15. Here's a fact: The train was late arriving in Chicago.
    Which one of the following items is relevant to the fact?
    a. Grace travels by train every summer.
    b. The train had fourteen passenger cars.
    c. The train left New York three hours late.

In the passage below, the sentences are numbered. Read the passage. Then answer items 16–18.

(1) Tom hailed the outcast. "Hello, Huckleberry."
(2) "Hello, yourself."
(3) "What's that you got?"
(4) "Dead rat."
(5) "Lemme see him, Huck. My, he's pretty stiff. Where'd you get him?"
(6) "Bought him off a boy."
(7) "What did you give?"
(8) "I give a blue marble."
(9) "Where'd you get the blue marble?"
(10) "Bought it off Ben Rogers two weeks ago for a lucky rabbit's foot."

16. Which character says sentence 3?
    a. Tom
    b. Huck
    c. Ben

17. Which character says sentence 8?
    a. Tom
    b. Huck
    c. Ben

18. In sentence 6, to what does the word him refer?
    a. Ben
    b. Tom
    c. The dead rat

Read the passage below. Then answer items 19–24.

About half past nine or ten o'clock, Tom returned to the deserted street to where the Adored Unknown Girl lived. He paused a moment. No sound fell upon his listening ear. A candle was casting a dull glow upon the curtain of a second-story window. Was the Adored Unknown Girl there? He climbed the fence and tiptoed through the plants until he stood under that window. He looked up at it long, and with emotion.

Tom lay down on his back under the window. His hands were folded on his chest, holding his poor wilted flower. As he lay there, Tom imagined that he would look this way if he were dying, with no shelter over his head, no loving face to bend over him. And thus she would see him when she looked out in the morning. Would she drop one little tear upon his poor, lifeless form? Would she heave one little sigh to see a bright young life so rudely cut down?

The window went up, a maidservant's voice broke the calm, and a torrent of water drenched poor Tom and brought him back to life. Tom sprang up with a snort, went over the fence, and shot away in the gloom.

Later that night, Polly mentioned that Jeff Thatcher's cousin Becky had moved to Saint Petersburg. Tom said nothing.

19. What time did Tom go to Becky's house?
    a. About half past nine in the evening
    b. About half past nine in the morning
    c. About half past six in the evening

20. What is the name of the Adored Unknown Girl?
    a. Her name is not given in the passage.
    b. Polly
    c. Becky

21. Where did the maid throw the water?
    a. Into the street
    b. Over the fence
    c. Through the open window

114   Reading Mastery Plus, Level 6

22. What emotion was Tom feeling as he looked up at the window?

  a. Jealousy
  ⓑ Adoration
  c. Depression

23. What will Tom probably do next?

  ⓐ Try to see the Adored Unknown Girl again
  b. Ask Polly about the Adored Unknown Girl
  c. Throw water at the maid

24. Why did Tom say nothing at the end of the passage?

  a. He was pretending to be dead again.
  b. He was in trouble for getting home late.
  ⓒ He didn't want anyone to know that he liked the girl.

Lessons 101–110

25. How did Aunt Polly know that Tom had been out at night?

  ⓐ Sid was awake when Tom came home and told her.
  b. It was on the morning news.
  c. Tom's nose grew when she asked him.

26. Who told a lie about the murder to save himself?

  a. The schoolmaster
  b. Dr. Robinson
  ⓒ Outlaw Joe

27. In the following sentence, the star shows where a word is missing.

Two dogs were on the stage when the whistle blew, but most * were still with their owners.

  a. owners
  b. stages
  ⓒ dogs

Look at the map below. Then answer items 28–30.

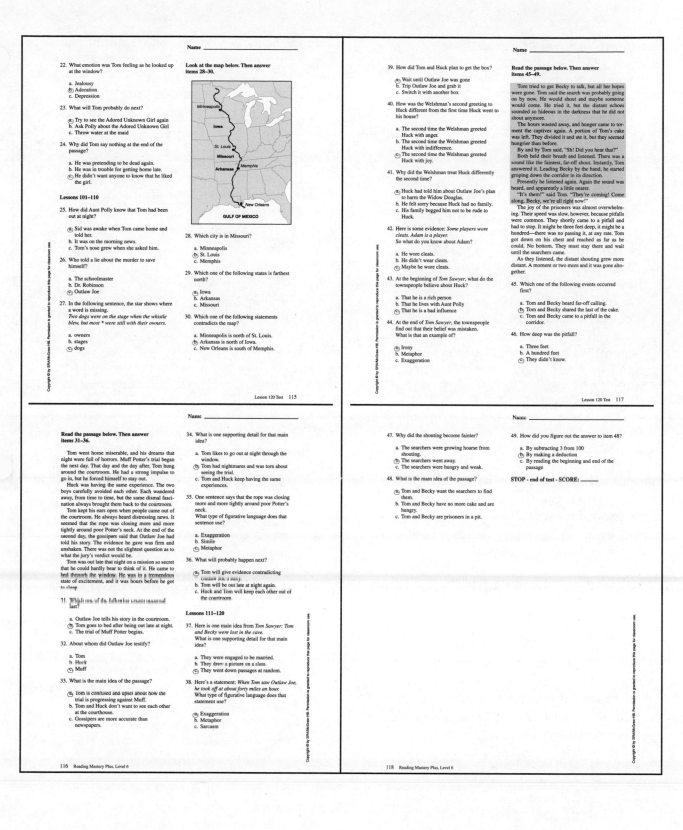

28. Which city is in Missouri?

  a. Minneapolis
  ⓑ St. Louis
  c. Memphis

29. Which one of the following states is farthest north?

  ⓐ Iowa
  b. Arkansas
  c. Missouri

30. Which one of the following statements contradicts the map?

  a. Minneapolis is north of St. Louis.
  ⓑ Arkansas is north of Iowa.
  c. New Orleans is south of Memphis.

Read the passage below. Then answer items 31–36.

Tom went home miserable, and his dreams that night were full of horrors. Muff Potter's trial began the next day. That day and the day after, Tom hung around the courtroom. He had a strong impulse to go in, but he forced himself to stay out.

Huck was having the same experience. The two boys carefully avoided each other. Each wandered away, from time to time, but the same dismal fascination always brought them back to the courtroom.

Tom kept his ears open when people came out of the courtroom. He always heard distressing news. It seemed that the rope was closing more and more tightly around poor Potter's neck. At the end of the second day, the gossipers said that Outlaw Joe had told his story. The evidence he gave was firm and unshaken. There was not the slightest question as to what the jury's verdict would be.

Tom was out late that night on a mission so secret that he could hardly bear to think of it. He came to bed through the window. He was in a tremendous state of excitement, and it was hours before he got to sleep.

31. Which one of the following events occurred last?

  a. Outlaw Joe tells his story in the courtroom.
  ⓑ Tom goes to bed after being out late at night.
  c. The trial of Muff Potter begins.

32. About whom did Outlaw Joe testify?

  a. Tom
  b. Huck
  ⓒ Muff

33. What is the main idea of the passage?

  ⓐ Tom is confused and upset about how the trial is progressing against Muff.
  b. Tom and Huck don't want to see each other at the courthouse.
  c. Gossipers are more accurate than newspapers.

34. What is one supporting detail for that main idea?

  a. Tom likes to go out at night through the window.
  ⓑ Tom had nightmares and was torn about seeing the trial.
  c. Tom and Huck keep having the same experiences.

35. One sentence says that the rope was closing more and more tightly around poor Potter's neck.
What type of figurative language does that sentence use?

  a. Exaggeration
  b. Simile
  ⓒ Metaphor

36. What will probably happen next?

  ⓐ Tom will give evidence contradicting Outlaw Joe's story.
  b. Tom will be out late at night again.
  c. Huck and Tom will keep each other out of the courtroom.

Lessons 111–120

37. Here is one main idea from *Tom Sawyer*: *Tom and Becky were lost in the cave.*
What is one supporting detail for that main idea?

  a. They were engaged to be married.
  b. They drew a picture on a slate.
  ⓒ They went down passages at random.

38. Here's a statement: *When Tom saw Outlaw Joe, he took off at about forty miles an hour.*
What type of figurative language does that statement use?

  ⓐ Exaggeration
  b. Metaphor
  c. Sarcasm

---

39. How did Tom and Huck plan to get the box?

  ⓐ Wait until Outlaw Joe was gone
  b. Trip Outlaw Joe and grab it
  c. Switch it with another box

40. How was the Welshman's second greeting to Huck different from the first time Huck went to his house?

  a. The second time the Welshman greeted Huck with anger.
  b. The second time the Welshman greeted Huck with indifference.
  ⓒ The second time the Welshman greeted Huck with joy.

41. Why did the Welshman treat Huck differently the second time?

  ⓐ Huck had told him about Outlaw Joe's plan to harm the Widow Douglas.
  b. He felt sorry because Huck had no family.
  c. His family begged him not to be rude to Huck.

42. Here is some evidence: *Some players wore cleats. Adam is a player.*
So what do you know about Adam?

  a. He wore cleats.
  b. He didn't wear cleats.
  ⓒ Maybe he wore cleats.

43. At the beginning of *Tom Sawyer*, what do the townspeople believe about Huck?

  a. That he is a rich person
  b. That he lives with Aunt Polly
  ⓒ That he is a bad influence

44. At the end of *Tom Sawyer*, the townspeople find out that their belief was mistaken. What is that an example of?

  ⓐ Irony
  b. Metaphor
  c. Exaggeration

Read the passage below. Then answer items 45–49.

Tom tried to get Becky to talk, but all her hopes were gone. Tom said the search was probably going on by now. He would shout and maybe someone would come. He tried it, but the distant echoes sounded so hideous in the darkness that he did not shout anymore.

The hours wasted away, and hunger came to torment the captives again. A portion of Tom's cake was left. They divided it and ate it, but they seemed hungrier than before.

By and by Tom said, "Sh! Did you hear that?" Both held their breath and listened. There was a sound like the faintest, far-off shout. Instantly, Tom answered it. Leading Becky by the hand, he started groping down the corridor in its direction.

Presently he listened again. Again the sound was heard, and apparently a little nearer.

"It's them!" said Tom. "They're coming! Come along, Becky, we're all right now!"

The joy of the prisoners was almost overwhelming. Their speed was slow, however, because pitfalls were common. They shortly came to a pitfall and had to stop. It might be three feet deep, it might be a hundred—there was no passing it, at any rate. Tom got down on his chest and reached as far as he could. No bottom. They must stay there and wait until the searchers came.

As they listened, the distant shouting grew more distant. A moment or two more and it was gone altogether.

45. Which one of the following events occurred first?

  a. Tom and Becky heard far-off calling.
  ⓑ Tom and Becky shared the last of the cake.
  c. Tom and Becky came to a pitfall in the corridor.

46. How deep was the pitfall?

  a. Three feet
  b. A hundred feet
  ⓒ They didn't know.

---

47. Why did the shouting become fainter?

  a. The searchers were growing hoarse from shouting.
  ⓑ The searchers went away.
  c. The searchers were hungry and weak.

48. What is the main idea of the passage?

  ⓐ Tom and Becky want the searchers to find them.
  b. Tom and Becky have no more cake and are hungry.
  c. Tom and Becky are prisoners in a pit.

49. How did you figure out the answer to item 48?

  a. By subtracting 3 from 100
  ⓑ By making a deduction
  c. By reading the beginning and end of the passage

STOP - end of test - SCORE: _____

Recording Individual Results

(Use the following script to record individual results.)

1. Look at your Individual Skills Profile Chart.
2. You're going to record your test results for lesson 120. First look at the test to find out which items you got wrong. Then circle those items on the chart.
3. Now record your results. I'll help you if you have any questions. (Circulate among the students as they record their results.)
4. (After the students finish, say:) Now count the items you did *not* circle and write the total in the **Total** box near the bottom of the column. The total should be the same as your test score.
5. Now you'll fill in the other boxes for lesson 120. If you scored 0 to 39 points, write an **X** in the box marked **Retest.** If you scored 40 to 49 points, write your score in the box marked **FINAL SCORE.**

Remedial Exercises

Students who scored 0 to 39 points on the test should be given remedial help. After the regular reading period is over, assemble these students and present the following exercises. The students will need their original test papers.

EXERCISE 1   Vocabulary Review

1. Let's talk about the meanings of some words.

2. The first word is **mortified.** When part of your body is dead, that part is **mortified.**
   - Everybody, what's another way of saying **Frostbite can cause your toes to become dead**? (Signal.) *Frostbite can cause your toes to become mortified.*

3. The next word is **vicious.** When something is **vicious,** it is cruel or violent.
   - Everybody, what's another way of saying **Siccing the dog on her was a cruel act**? (Signal.) *Siccing the dog on her was a vicious act.*

4. The next word is **tranquil. Tranquil** is another word for **calm.**
   - Everybody, what's another way of saying **Even when the students are noisy, our teacher is always calm**? (Signal.) *Even when the students are noisy, our teacher is always tranquil.*

5. The next word is **crestfallen.** When you are **crestfallen,** you are ashamed or humiliated.
   - Everybody, what's another way of saying **I was humiliated when I broke the vase**? (Signal.) *I was crestfallen when I broke the vase.*

6. The next word is **indifferent.** When you are **indifferent** about something, you don't care about that thing.
   - Everybody, what's another way of saying **She didn't care about the color of the walls**? (Signal.) *She was indifferent about the color of the walls.*

7. The next word is **immortal.** Something that is **immortal** lives forever.
   - Everybody, what's another way of saying **That legend lives forever**? (Signal.) *That legend is immortal.*

8. The next word is **revive.** When something **revives,** it comes back to life or to a healthy state.
   - Everybody, what's another way of saying **After the long hike, the cool water helped us come back to life**? (Signal.) *After the long hike, the cool water helped us revive.*

9. The next word is **resemble.** When something **resembles** another thing, it looks like that other thing.
   - Everybody, what's another way of saying **Do the twins look like each other**? (Signal.) *Do the twins resemble each other?*

10. The next word is **elude. Elude** is another word for **avoid.**
    - Everybody, what's another way of saying **When you play tag, you avoid the person who is "it"**? (Signal.) *When you play tag, you elude the person who is "it."*

11. The next word is **loft. Loft** is another word for **attic.**
    - Everybody, what's another way of saying **We built a playhouse in the attic**? (Signal.) *We built a playhouse in the loft.*

12. The next word is **inlet. An inlet** is a small bay.
    - Everybody, what's another of saying **We sailed the boat into a small bay**? (Signal.) *We sailed the boat into an inlet.*

13. The next word is **bluff. A bluff** is a high, steep riverbank or cliff.
    - Everybody, what's another way of saying **Are there many cliffs along the Missouri River**? (Signal.) *Are there many bluffs along the Missouri River?*

14. The next word is **deputy. A deputy** is an assistant.
    - Everybody, what's another way of saying **Our club elected me assistant treasurer**? (Signal.) *Our club elected me deputy treasurer.*

15. The next word is **sentry. A sentry** is a guard.
    - Everybody, what's another way of saying **The guard stood as still as a statue**? (Signal.) *The sentry stood as still as a statue.*

16. The next word is **scoundrel.** Someone who is a **scoundrel** is a mean or evil person.
    - Everybody, what's another way of saying **The villain in the book was an evil person**? (Signal.) *The villain in the book was a scoundrel.*

17. The next word is **impact. Impact** is another word for **effect.**
    - Everybody, what's another way of saying **Did the book have an effect on you?** (Signal.) *Did the book have an impact on you?*

18. The next word is **relic. A relic** is something left over from the past.
    - Everybody, what's another way of saying **These arrowheads are left over from the past**? (Signal.) *These arrowheads are relics.*

19. The next word is **catastrophe. Catastrophe** is another word for **disaster.**
    - Everybody, what's another way of saying **The sirens warned of a disaster**? (Signal.) *The sirens warned of a catastrophe.*

20. The next word is **juvenile. A juvenile** is a young person.
    - Everybody, what's another way of saying **My sister is a young person**? (Signal.) *My sister is a juvenile.*

21. The next word is **flustered. Flustered** is another word for **confused.**
    - Everybody, what's another way of saying **I get confused on this freeway**? (Signal.) *I get flustered on this freeway.*

22. The next word is **stalactite. A stalactite** is a type of rock that hangs from the ceiling of a cave.
    - Everybody, what's another way of saying **A rock that hangs from the ceiling of a cave looks like an icicle**? (Signal.) *A stalactite looks like an icicle.*

23. The next word is **famished.** When you are **famished,** you are very hungry.
    - Everybody, what's another way of saying **He was very hungry by noon**? (Signal.) *He was famished by noon.*

24. The next word is **hamlet. A hamlet** is a small village.
    - Everybody, what's another way of saying **The story was set in a small village in England**? (Signal.) *The story was set in a hamlet in England.*

25. The last word is **furnish.** When something is **furnished,** it is supplied.
    - Everybody, what's another way of saying **Could you please supply the drinks for the picnic?** (Signal.) *Could you please furnish the drinks for the picnic?*

EXERCISE 2   General Review

1. Who was Outlaw Joe? (Idea: *The grave robber who killed Dr. Robinson.*)
   - Who was Huckleberry Finn? (Idea: *The juvenile outcast of the village—admired because he didn't have to go to school.*)
   - Who was Aunt Polly? (Idea: *Tom's dead mother's sister with whom Tom and Sid lived.*)

2. What did Huck say could cure warts? (Idea: *Dead rats.*)
   - What did Tom say could cure warts? (Idea: *Stump water.*)

3. Here's a fact: *Janet got a cookbook for her birthday.*
   - Here's an item: *Janet likes to cook.*
   - Does that item help explain the fact? (Response: *Yes.*)
   - So is that item **relevant** or **irrelevant**? (Response: *Relevant.*)

4. Everybody, look at the passage in the left column on page 114 of your test. (**Call on a student to read the passage aloud.**)
   - Which character says sentence 2? (Response: *Huck.*)
   - Which character says sentence 6? (Response: *Huck.*)
   - Which character says sentence 7? (Response: *Tom.*)
   - In sentence 5, to whom does the word *you* refer? (Response: *Huck.*)

5. When Tom sneaked in through his bedroom window, he thought nobody knew he had been gone. But who was awake? (Response: *Sid.*)

6. Which character actually killed Dr. Robinson and blamed it on Muff Potter? (Response: *Outlaw Joe.*)

7. Here's a sentence: *Mom was here, but Dad wasn't here.*
   - Here's the same sentence with a word missing: *Mom was here, but Dad wasn't.*
   - What word is missing? (Response: *Here.*)

8. Everybody, look at the map on page 115 of your test.
   - Which state is above Arkansas? (Response: *Missouri.*)
   - Which state is above Missouri? (Response: *Iowa.*)
   - Which city is between Minneapolis and Memphis? (Response: *St. Louis.*)

9. I'll make some statements about the map. Tell me if each statement is **contradictory** or **not contradictory.**
   - St. Louis is north of Minneapolis. (Response: *Contradictory.*)
   - Missouri is south of Iowa. (Response: *Not contradictory.*)

10. Here is a main idea from the novel *Tom Sawyer: Tom and Huck went to the graveyard.*
    - Name some supporting details for that main idea. (Ideas: *They wanted to get rid of warts; they went at midnight; they saw the grave robbers; they saw the murder.*)

11. Here's a statement: *My suitcase weighs a ton.*
    - What type of figurative language does that statement use? (Response: *Exaggeration.*)
    - How much does a suitcase really weigh? (Idea: *A lot.*)

12. How did the Welshman greet Huck the first time Huck went to his house? (Idea: *With suspicion.*)
    - What did Huck tell the Welshman? (Idea: *About Outlaw Joe's plan to harm Widow Douglas.*)

13. What did the Welshman and his sons do? (Idea: *They saved her.*)
    - How did the Welshman greet Huck the second time Huck went to his house? (Idea: *With a great welcome.*)

14. Here is some evidence: *Some trees are tall. We have a tree.*
    - So what do you know about our tree? (Idea: *Maybe it's tall.*)

15. Who was Huck Finn's father? (Idea: *The town bum.*)
    - Did the townspeople allow their children to play with Huck? (Response: *No.*)

- Why or why not? (Idea: *They thought he was lazy and bad*.)

EXERCISE 3   Passage Reading

Passage 1

1. Everybody, look at the passage in the right column on page 114 of your test. You're going to read the passage aloud.

2. (Call on individual students to read several sentences each. Correct any decoding errors. When the students finish, present the following questions.)

3. What time did Tom go to the house of the girl? (Idea: *About half past nine or ten*.)
   - What was burning in the window? (Response: *A candle*.)
   - Was it day or night? (Response: *Night*.)

4. What does Tom call the girl? (Response: *The Adored Unknown Girl*.)
   - Why doesn't he call her by name? (Idea: *He doesn't know it*.)
   - Who just moved to town? (Ideas: *The girl; Becky*.)

5. What did Tom climb over to get into the yard? (Idea: *A fence*.)
   - Where did he lie with his flower? (Idea: *Under a window*.)
   - From where did the maid throw the water? (Idea: *From the window*.)

6. How did Tom imagine the girl would look at him if she saw him dying? (Idea: *Lovingly*.)

7. Did Tom tell anyone about his experience at the girl's house or how he felt about her? (Response: *No*.)

Passage 2

1. Everybody, look at the passage on page 116 of your test. You're going to read the passage aloud.

2. (Call on individual students to read several sentences each. Correct any decoding errors. When the students finish, present the following questions.)

3. Did Outlaw Joe tell his story in court *before* or *after* Tom was out late at night? (Idea: *Before*.)

4. Who was on trial? (Response: *Muff Potter*.)

5. I'll read a paragraph from the passage. "Tom was out late that night on a mission so secret that he could hardly bear to think of it. He came to bed through the window. He was in a tremendous state of excitement, and it was hours before he got to sleep."
   - The paragraph mentions how Tom feels after being out on a secret mission. How does he feel? (Idea: *So excited he couldn't sleep*.)
   - So what's the main idea of the paragraph? (Idea: *Tom was so excited after his secret mission he couldn't sleep*.)

6. Here's a sentence: *The little girl was prancing around in her new dress at the wedding.*
   - What is the little girl being compared to? (Idea: *A horse*.)
   - So what kind of figurative language does that sentence use? (Response: *Metaphor*.)

7. What do you think Tom will do about Outlaw Joe's testimony, which seems so firm? (Idea: *Give his side of the story*.)

Passage 3

1. Everybody, look at the passage on page 117 of your test. You're going to read the passage aloud.

2. (Call on individual students to read several sentences each. Correct any decoding errors. When the students finish, present the following questions.)

3. Did Tom and Becky eat the cake *before* or *after* they heard the shouts? (Response: *Before*.)

4. What did Tom do when they came to the pitfall? (Idea: *He got down and tried to touch the bottom*.)
   - Could he reach the bottom? (Response: *No*.)
   - So does he know how deep the pitfall is? (Response: *No*.)

5. Does a sound get stronger or weaker as the object making the sound moves farther away? (Response: *Weaker.*)

6. Everybody, look at the first paragraph in the right column on page 117 of your test. (Call on a student to read the first paragraph.)
   - Who are the main characters in that paragraph? (Idea: *Tom and Becky.*)
   - What is the main thing they do? (Ideas: *Tom tried to keep up Becky's hopes by telling her a search was probably going on; Tom shouted for someone to come.*)
   - So what's the main idea? (Idea: *Tom tried to keep up Becky's hopes.*)

Retesting the Students

After you've completed the remedial exercises, retest each student individually. To administer the retest, you will need the student's original test paper, a blank copy of the test, and a red pencil. Give the student the blank copy of the test. Say, "Look at page 113. You're going to take this test again. Read each item aloud and tell me the answer."

Use the student's original test paper to grade the retest. Use the red pencil to mark each correct answer with a **C** and each incorrect answer with an **X**. Then count one point for each correct answer and write the new score at the bottom of the page. Finally, revise the Individual Skills Profile Chart by drawing an **X** over any items the student missed on the retest.

Complete the Group Point Chart for lesson 120.

Administering the Checkouts

You can conduct checkouts by using the passage on page 117 of the Lesson 120 Mastery Test. See page 9 for a complete description of checkout procedures.

Tested Skills and Concepts

The Lesson 120 Mastery Test measures student mastery of the following skills and concepts.

- using vocabulary words in context (items 1–6)
- using context to predict word meaning (items 7–12)
- recalling details and events (items 13 and 43)
- identifying literal cause and effect (item 14)
- identifying relevant evidence (item 15)
- interpreting extended dialogues (items 16 and 17)
- interpreting substitute words (item 18)
- answering literal questions about a text (items 19 and 46)
- inferring story details and events (items 20 and 32)
- distinguishing settings by features (item 21)
- interpreting a character's feelings (item 22)
- predicting a character's actions (item 23)
- drawing conclusions (item 24)
- inferring causes and effects (items 25 and 47)
- distinguishing characters by trait (item 26)
- interpreting combined sentences (item 27)
- interpreting maps (items 28 and 29)
- identifying contradictions (item 30)
- sequencing narrative events (items 31 and 45)
- inferring the main idea (items 33 and 48)
- inferring details relevant to a main idea (items 34 and 37)
- interpreting figurative language (items 35 and 38)
- predicting narrative outcomes (item 36)
- evaluating problems and solutions (item 39)
- making comparisons (item 40)
- inferring a character's point of view (item 41)
- completing written deductions (item 42)
- interpreting irony (item 44)
- identifying inferential questions (item 49)

Interpreting Test Results

The test results are recorded on the Individual Skills Profile Chart, the Group Point Chart, and the Writing Assessment Chart. Each chart gives a different interpretation of the results. The Individual Skills Profile Chart shows the specific skills the students have mastered; the Group Point Chart shows the group's overall performance; the Writing Assessment Chart gives students a place to record their writing scores.

The Individual Skills Profile Chart

The Individual Skills Profile Chart should be used to assess each student's strengths and weaknesses. Test items the student missed on an initial test will be circled; items missed on a retest will be crossed out. On the sample chart below, the student took a retest on lesson 20. Note that some items have been both circled and crossed out for lesson 20.

If a chart has a great many items that are circled or crossed out, the student may still be weak in certain areas. Look for two general patterns of weakness. In the first pattern, a student will consistently fail items that measure a particular skill. On the sample chart below, for example, the student consistently failed items that measured the skill "inferring causes and effects." Students who fall into this pattern may require further teaching of particular skills.

In the second pattern, a student will do poorly on one test but fairly well on the other tests. On the sample chart below, for example, the student did poorly on the test for lesson 20. Usually, students who fall into this pattern were absent on the days preceding the test. These students may profit from a review of the lessons they missed.

Individual Skills Profile Chart A   Name Sample

Skills	Tests	10	20	30	40	50	60
Comprehension Skills							
using vocabulary words in context		1 2 3	1 2 3	1, 2, 3, 4, 5, 6	1 2 3	1 2 3	1, 2, 3, 4, 5, 6
using context to predict word meaning		4 5 6	4 5 6	7, 8, 9, 10, 11, 12	4 5 6	4 5 6	7, 8, 9, 10, 11, 12
answering literal questions about a text		15		27, 36		15	19, 31
identifying literal cause and effect		11	7	13, 25	9		20, 52
recalling details and events		7		23, 38	8		25, 40
sequencing narrative events		14	11	18, 28 44, 46		16	37
predicting narrative outcomes							24, 50
inferring causes and effects		(12)		26, 43	(4)		21, 40
inferring causes and effects		8		24, 48			23
making comparisons			8	22	7		14, 38
inferring the main idea				19		12	34
inferring details relevant to a main idea				10	20	11	13	18, 35, 44
completing written deductions							27, 46
drawing conclusions		9		31, 32		17	39, 53
evaluating problems and solutions		10		16, 30	13		15, 42
identifying relevant evidence				32, 33, 34, 35			16, 17
identifying contradictions							29, 30
identifying inferential questions							47, 49
identifying logical fallacies							
Literary Skills							
interpreting a character's feelings				14, 17	12		26
interpreting a character's motives				15, 29	16		21
inferring a character's point of view		13		40		(4)	43, 51
predicting a character's actions				47	14		36
distinguishing settings by features		16	12	41	10		22
distinguishing characters by trait			14	21, 39	17		13, 41
interpreting figurative language				42 45		7, 8, 9, 10, 11	28, 37, 45
Total		14	11	44	16	16	51
Retest			X				
FINAL SCORE		14	12	44	16	16	51

Individual Skills Profile Chart A

Name _____

	Skills	Tests	10	20	30	40	50	60
Comprehension Skills	using vocabulary words in context		1 2 3	1 2 3	1, 2, 3, 4, 5, 6	1 2 3	1 2 3	1, 2, 3, 4, 5, 6
	using context to predict word meaning		4 5 6	4 5 6	7, 8, 9, 10, 11, 12	4 5 6	4 5 6	7, 8, 9, 10, 11, 12
	answering literal questions about a text		15		27, 36		15	19, 31
	identifying literal cause and effect		11	7	13, 25	9		20, 52
	recalling details and events		7		23, 38	8		25, 40
	sequencing narrative events		14	11	18, 28		16	32
	predicting narrative outcomes				44, 46			24, 50
	inferring causes and effects		12		26, 43			33, 48
	inferring story details and events		8		24, 48	15		23
	making comparisons			8	22	7		14, 38
	inferring the main idea			9	19		12	34
	inferring details relevant to a main idea			10	20	11	13	18, 35, 44
	completing written deductions							27, 46
	drawing conclusions		9		31, 37		17	39, 53
	evaluating problems and solutions		10		16, 30	13		15, 42
	identifying relevant evidence				32, 33, 34, 35			16, 17
	identifying contradictions							29, 30
	identifying inferential questions							47, 49
	identifying logical fallacies							
Literary Skills	interpreting a character's feelings			16	14, 17	12		26
	interpreting a character's motives			13	15, 29	16		21
	inferring a character's point of view		13		40		14	43, 51
	predicting a character's actions			15	47	14		36
	distinguishing settings by features		16	12	41	10		22
	distinguishing characters by trait			14	21, 39	17		13, 41
	interpreting figurative language				42 45		7, 8, 9, 10, 11	28, 37, 45
	Total							
	Retest							
	FINAL SCORE							

Individual Skills Profile Chart B

Name _____

	Skills	Tests	70	80	90	100	110	120
Comprehension Skills	using vocabulary words in context		1, 2, 3, 4	1, 2, 3, 4	1, 2, 3, 4, 5, 6	1, 2, 3, 4	1, 2, 3, 4	1, 2, 3, 4, 5, 6
	using context to predict word meaning		5, 6, 7, 8	5, 6, 7, 8	7, 8, 9, 10, 11, 12	5, 6, 7, 8	5, 6, 7, 8,	7, 8, 9, 10, 11, 12
	answering literal questions about a text				20, 31, 48		22	19 46
	identifying literal cause and effect				50	18		14
	recalling details and events			14	37, 39	17	9	13, 43
	sequencing narrative events		22	18	25, 49			31, 45
	predicting narrative outcomes		23			20		36
	inferring causes and effects				33, 38	19		25, 47
	inferring story details and events		18	20	21		19	20, 32
	making comparisons			23	26, 42			40
	inferring the main idea		20	16	36	22		33, 48
	inferring details relevant to a main idea		21	12	43			34, 37
	completing written deductions				45	9		42
	drawing conclusions			15	23		10	24
	evaluating problems and solutions				41	13		39
	identifying relevant evidence			10	44			15
	identifying contradictions		14		19	16		30
	identifying inferential questions			17	46	23		49
	identifying logical fallacies						13, 14	
Literary Skills	interpreting a character's feelings			19	53		20	22
	interpreting a character's motives		9	21	51		21	
	inferring a character's point of view		10		34	21		41
	predicting a character's actions			22	35		24	23
	distinguishing settings by features			13	52	14		21
	distinguishing characters by trait		19		22			26
	interpreting figurative language		13	11, 24	14, 15, 16, 32	15	23	35, 38
	interpreting extended dialogues		15, 16		28, 29			16, 17
	interpreting substitute words		17		24, 30			18
	interpreting shortened sentences		11, 12		27	10	11	
	interpreting combined sentences			9	47	11	12	27
	interpreting irony				40			44
Study Skills	interpreting maps				17, 18			28, 29
	filling out forms						15, 16	
	identifying proper reference sources				13	12		
	interpreting graphs						17, 18	
	Total							
	Retest							
	FINAL SCORE							

The Group Point Chart

The Group Point Chart should be used to assess the group's overall performance. Before interpreting the Group Point Chart, it is necessary to complete the final two columns of the chart for each student.

1. Add the scores in the **left** side of each box and enter the total in the column labeled "checkouts."

2. Add the scores in the **right** side of each box and enter the total in the column labeled "tests."

The completed sample chart below shows each student's final totals for the checkouts and the mastery tests.

Because the checkouts and the mastery tests measure different types of skills, you should evaluate each total separately.

The checkouts measure decoding skills. The students can earn a maximum of 24 points on the checkouts (2 points for each checkout). Students who score 8 to 24 points on the checkouts have probably mastered the decoding skills taught in the program.

The mastery tests measure comprehension skills, literary skills, and study skills. The students can earn a maximum of 363 points on the twelve mastery tests. Students who score 291 to 363 points on the mastery tests have probably mastered the comprehension, literary, and study skills taught in the program.

Group Point Chart A

Names / Lessons	10	20	30	40	50	60	check-outs	tests
Suzy Abrams	2 / 16	2 / 15	2 / 48	2 / 17	2 / 15	2 / 52	12	163
Alan Bannister	0 / 13	2 / 12	2 / 38	2 / 13	0 / 15	2 / 48	8	139
Lupe Calderon	0 / 12	0 / 14	2 / 40	2 / 15	0 / 15	2 / 50	6	146

Group Point Chart A

Names	Lessons	10	20	30	40	50	60		check-outs	tests

Group Point Chart B

Names	Lessons	70	80	90	100	110	120		check-outs	tests

72   Reading Mastery Plus, Level 6, Testing and Management Handbook

Copyrigh   SRA/McGraw-Hill. Permission is granted to reproduce this page for classroom use.

Writing Assessment Chart

Name _____

Test	Score	Ways to Improve
10		
20		
30		
40		
50		
60		
70		
80		
90		
100		
110		
120		

Placement Test

Name _____

PART 1

The Golden Touch

Once upon a time in ancient Turkey there lived a rich king named Midas, who had a daughter named Marygold.

King Midas was very fond of gold. The only thing he loved more was his daughter. But the more Midas loved his daughter, the more he desired gold. He thought the best thing he could possibly do for his child would be to give her the largest pile of yellow, glistening coins that had ever been heaped together since the world began. So Midas gave all his thoughts and all his time to collecting gold.

When Midas gazed at the gold-tinted clouds of sunset, he wished they were real gold and that they could be herded into his strong box. When little Marygold ran to meet him with a bunch of buttercups and dandelions, he used to say, "Pooh, pooh, child. If these flowers were as golden as they look, they would be worth picking."

And yet, in his earlier days, before he had this insane desire for gold, Midas had shown a great love for flowers. He had planted a garden with the biggest and sweetest roses any person ever saw or smelled. These roses were still growing in the garden, as large, as lovely, and as fragrant as they were when Midas used to pass whole hours looking at them and inhaling their perfume. But now, if he looked at the flowers at all, it was only to calculate how much the garden would be worth if each of the rose petals was a thin plate of gold.

PART 2

1. *Circle the answer.* What kind of royal person was Midas?

   • an emperor   • a king   • a prince

2. *Circle the answer.* So his daughter was __.

   • an empress   • a queen   • a princess

3. What did Midas love most of all?

   _____

4. What did he love almost as much?

   _____

5. The more Midas loved _____,

   the more he desired _____.

6. Why did Midas think that dandelions were not worth picking?

   _____

7. What kind of flowers had Midas planted in his earlier days?

   _____

8. Midas used to inhale the _____
   of those flowers.

9. What did Midas think about his garden now?

   _____

Lesson 10

Sample Items

1. Several cows were <u>grazing</u> in the pasture.
   a. eating plants
   b. running around
   c. sleeping

2. What was the name of Homer's uncle?
   a. Odysseus
   b. Ulysses
   c. Mr. Gabby

For items 1–6, circle the letter of the answer that means the same thing as the underlined part.

1. The auto accident was a great <u>misfortune</u>.

   a. calamity
   b. mist
   c. peril

2. No one <u>died</u> during the big earthquake.

   a. enlarged
   b. cherished
   c. perished

3. The boy was <u>suspicious</u> of the free offer.

   a. advanced
   b. hideous
   c. skeptical

4. The can opener is a useful <u>gadget</u>.

   a. weapon
   b. device
   c. metal

5. The roaring elephants made a <u>commotion</u> at the zoo.

   a. rodeo
   b. sculpture
   c. disturbance

6. The traveler <u>encountered</u> a dog and began to pet it.

   a. came into contact with
   b. followed closely
   c. chased

For items 7–16, circle the letter of the correct answer.

7. What was the name of Odysseus's son?

   a. Hermes
   b. Telemachus
   c. Polyphemus

Read the passage below. Then answer items 8–10.

People had begun to gather outside the lunch room window, and someone was saying, "There are almost as many doughnuts as there are people in Centerburg, and I wonder how in tarnation Ulysses thinks he can sell all of 'em!"

Every once in a while somebody would come inside and buy some, but while somebody bought two to eat and a dozen to take home, the machine made three dozen more.

By the time Uncle Ulysses and the sheriff arrived and pushed through the crowd, the lunch room was a calamity of doughnuts!

8. How did the people know there were a lot of doughnuts?

   a. They heard about the doughnuts from the sheriff.
   b. They saw the sandwich sign man.
   c. They saw the doughnuts through the lunch room window.

9. Why did the author call the lunch room "a calamity of doughnuts"?

   a. The machine made doughnuts faster than people bought them.
   b. The doughnuts were stacked too high.
   c. The sheriff didn't like doughnuts.

10. How could Uncle Ulysses solve the problem of too many doughnuts?

   a. Have a doughnut sale
   b. Open the window
   c. Close the store

Read the passage below. Then answer items 11–16.

To their joy, as Odysseus and his crew left Circe's island, a strong wind blew from the north, driving the ship south. Presently the wind fell, and the sea was calm. Nearby, they saw a beautiful island from which came the sound of sweet singing. Odysseus knew who the singers were, for Circe had told him. They were the Sirens—beautiful mermaids who were deadly to men. The Sirens sat and sang among the flowers, but the flowers hid the bones of men who had listened to their singing. The singing had enchanted these men and carried their souls away. They had landed on the island and died of that strange music.

Odysseus wanted to hear the Sirens. He took a great piece of wax and cut it up into small pieces, which he gave to his men. Then he ordered his men to bind him tightly to the mast with ropes and told them not to unbind him until after they had passed the Sirens.

After Odysseus was bound to the mast, he ordered his men to soften the wax and place it in their ears so they would not hear the Sirens. When all this was done, the men sat down on the benches and pulled their oars. The ship rushed along and soon came near the island.

Odysseus heard the sweet singing of the Sirens. They seemed to offer him all knowledge and wisdom, which they knew he loved more than anything else in the world. He wanted to go to their island, and he begged his men to loosen his ropes. But the men could not hear him, and they rowed the ship past the island until the song of the Sirens faded away. Then they set Odysseus free and took the wax out of their ears.

11. Why couldn't the men hear the Sirens?

   a. They were too far away.
   b. They had wax in their ears.
   c. The ocean made too much noise.

12. Why didn't Odysseus swim toward the Sirens?

   a. He had wax in his ears.
   b. His feet were in chains.
   c. He was tied to the mast.

13. Why did Odysseus like the Sirens so much?

   a. They seemed to offer him knowledge and wisdom.
   b. They were the most beautiful creatures he had ever seen.
   c. They carried his soul away to a beautiful place.

14. What was the first thing Odysseus ordered his men to do?

   a. Put wax in their ears
   b. Bind him to the mast
   c. Loosen his ropes

15. What did the flowers hide?

   a. The Sirens' tails
   b. Deadly plants
   c. The bones of men

16. In which place would you find rotting clothes?

   a. Circe's island
   b. The Sirens' island
   c. Odysseus's boat

STOP – end of test – SCORE: _____

Lesson 20

For items 1–6, circle the letter of the answer that means the same thing as the underlined part.

1. The details of the contract are his <u>business</u>.

   a. vow
   b. affair
   c. spoil

2. The child <u>smeared</u> the carpet with her sticky fingers.

   a. smudged
   b. neglected
   c. rotted

3. The young girl had a <u>confused</u> look on her face.

   a. courteous
   b. feeble
   c. bewildered

4. The <u>custom</u> of removing our shoes soon became a habit.

   a. state law
   b. company rule
   c. way of behaving

5. The <u>burro</u> was kept on a long rope.

   a. corn and beef casserole
   b. small donkey
   c. brightly colored bird

6. The woman used a <u>gourd</u> to dig holes to plant seeds.

   a. fruit with a hard shell
   b. tool with a wooden handle
   c. three-wheeled tractor

For items 7–16, circle the letter of the correct answer.

7. How did the beggar convince Penelope that he had really met Odysseus?

   a. He told her what Odysseus wore.
   b. He told her about a birthmark Odysseus had.
   c. He told her a secret password.

8. How is a mesa different from a mountain?

   a. A mesa comes out of the ground.
   b. A mesa can be rocky.
   c. A mesa has a flat top.

Read the paragraph below. Then answer items 9–10.

When the sides of the bowl were high enough, Grandmother took some dried pieces of gourd shell out of a basket. They were what she used for shaping the bowl. She took a piece that was curved just right and held it against the side of the bowl and pushed from inside, till it was shaped like the curve of the gourd.

9. What is the main idea of the paragraph?

   a. Grandmother used pieces of gourd shell.
   b. Grandmother took something out of a basket.
   c. Grandmother shaped the bowl.

10. What is one supporting detail for that main idea?

    a. Grandmother lived on a mesa.
    b. Grandmother had a basket.
    c. Grandmother pushed a gourd shell against the bowl.

Read the passage below. Then answer items 11–16.

Mother and Father knew they would need money to buy food next winter. There are jobs in summer when the tourists come to stay in the hotels, and my parents decided that my mother should get such a job to earn extra money.

I said, "But what will we do? Won't we go to the mesa? What will Grandmother do?"

Mother said, "Kate, you are big, you will help Grandmother. Johnny will do his share. He is big enough to bring wood and water. Perhaps the neighbors will help with Grandmother's garden. But if the mesa springs are as dry as ours, perhaps there will not be much of a garden. When the summer is over and we come to get you, perhaps Grandmother will come with us and live here."

I did not think she would, but I did not say so.

So my father drove us to the mesa in the truck. It is about forty miles. We rode across the desert, between red and black and yellow rocks, and sand dunes covered with sage and yellow-flowered rabbit-brush. I was thinking about the work I would do. I don't mind the work, because it's important. Someday Grandmother's house will be Mother's, and then it will be mine. So I ought to know how to do everything.

11. Which one of the following events occurred first?

   a. Father took Kate and Johnny to Grandmother's house.
   b. Mother told Kate to help Grandmother.
   c. Father and Mother decided that Mother should get a job in the summer.

12. In which place would you find colorful rocks?

   a. The mesa
   b. The desert
   c. The sand dunes

13. Why did Kate think they should go to Grandmother's house?

   a. To see the sand dunes
   b. To make Johnny work
   c. To help Grandmother

14. Which character encouraged Kate to help Grandmother?

   a. Mother
   b. Father
   c. Johnny

15. What will Kate do when she arrives at Grandmother's house?

   a. Help in the house and garden
   b. Watch television
   c. Make Johnny do all the work

16. How does Kate probably feel about helping Grandmother for the summer?

   a. She thinks she will be bored all summer.
   b. She feels sorry for herself.
   c. She feels proud for being in charge of important work.

STOP - end of test - SCORE: _____

Lesson 30

For items 1–12, circle the letter of the answer that means the same thing as the underlined part.

1. The manager was busy when I called, so the telephone operator told me to wait a minute.

   a. create a market
   b. sow the seeds of doom
   c. hold the wire

2. Her winter jacket was lined with the fur of a sheep.

   a. batter
   b. tar
   c. fleece

3. The entertainer tells stories and sings songs.

   a. suitor
   b. boar
   c. minstrel

4. The farmer tilled the garden with a tool used to break up dirt.

   a. hoe
   b. lasso
   c. squash

5. The painful illness made Dad a miserable person.

   a. goblin
   b. wretch
   c. mirage

6. The spoiled child showed disrespect to the babysitter.

   a. contempt
   b. one chance in ten
   c. palette

7. Liz took a risk when she tried out for the team.

   a. her turn
   b. a break
   c. a chance

8. The festival was held in the plaza.

   a. open area surrounded by walls or buildings
   b. apple or peach orchard
   c. petting area of a zoo

9. The army took revenge on the winner of the battle.

   a. sent a gift to
   b. got even with
   c. was proud of

10. Did you tether the dog with the chain as I asked?

    a. tie
    b. play with
    c. feed

11. The historic lunatic asylum is on the city tour.

    a. pool where manatees swim
    b. home where runaway slaves hid
    c. place where insane people are kept

12. The hunter is stalking quail in the desert.

    a. quietly following
    b. taking photographs of
    c. doing tricks with

For items 13–48, circle the letter of the correct answer.

Lessons 1–10

13. During the 1930s, why did unemployed people go from town to town?

    a. To write about their travels
    b. To look for work
    c. To visit other unemployed people

14. What did Aunt Agnes think Uncle Ulysses did with his spare time?

    a. Frittered it away
    b. Napped
    c. Ate doughnuts

15. What is the most likely reason Mr. Gabby came into the lunch room?

    a. He smelled the doughnuts.
    b. He knew Uncle Ulysses.
    c. He had nowhere else to go.

16. How did Homer solve the problem of the missing bracelet?

    a. By cutting all the doughnuts in half
    b. By advertising a reward for the bracelet
    c. By giving Mr. Gabby a job

Read the passage below. Then answer items 17–21.

As the years went by, most of the people of Ithaca came to believe that Odysseus must be dead. Only his wife, Penelope, his son, Telemachus, and a few of his servants thought he was still alive.

With Odysseus gone, the people of Ithaca no longer had a king. Telemachus was too young to become the king, and Penelope was not allowed to take her husband's place. But any man who married Penelope could become the new king.

Many men wanted to marry Penelope, but she refused them all. After a while, these men decided to join together and stay at Odysseus's palace until Penelope agreed to marry one of them. They were called suitors, and there were more than a hundred of them. They did nothing but eat all day long, and nobody could stop them. They would never go away, they said, until Penelope chose one of them to be her husband and king of the island.

Year after year, Penelope kept hoping that Odysseus was still alive and would return soon. Telemachus hoped so, too, although he worried about what the suitors might do if Odysseus did return. They might kill Odysseus, and then Penelope would be forced to marry one of them.

17. Why did most of the people of Ithaca think Odysseus must be dead?

    a. Because he had been gone for years
    b. Because Penelope believed he was dead
    c. Because his son said he saw him die

18. Which event happened last?

    a. Odysseus disappeared from Ithaca.
    b. Penelope's suitors decided to stay at the palace.
    c. Many men asked Penelope to marry them.

19. What is the main idea of the passage?

    a. The suitors ate all day long at the palace.
    b. Penelope was not allowed to take her husband's place as ruler.
    c. Because Odysseus was gone, many men wanted to marry Penelope.

20. What is one supporting detail for that main idea?

    a. Only Penelope, Telemachus, and a few servants thought Odysseus was still alive.
    b. There were more than a hundred suitors.
    c. The suitors might kill Odysseus if he returned.

21. Which character was worried about what the suitors might do if Odysseus returned?

    a. Telemachus
    b. Penelope
    c. Odysseus

Lessons 11–20

22. According to Athena what did the eagle's attack show?

    a. Odysseus will take revenge on the suitors.
    b. Odysseus will kill all the geese in the kingdom.
    c. Odysseus is as strong as an eagle.

23. How was Odysseus disguised?

    a. As an eagle
    b. As a beggar
    c. As Athena

24. Why did Argos make one last effort to stand before he died?

    a. The suitors ordered him to get up.
    b. He knew his master Odysseus.
    c. He wanted to show how he used to hunt.

25. How did the nurse know that the beggar was Odysseus?

    a. She recognized the long scar on his leg.
    b. He told her.
    c. Telemachus told her.

Read the passage below. Then answer items 26–31.

The suitors warmed and greased the bow, and one after another they tried to bend it. Meanwhile, Eumayus and the cow farmer went out into the court, and Odysseus followed them. He asked them, "Whose side would you two take if Odysseus came home? Would you fight for him or for the suitors?"

"For Odysseus!" they both cried. "If only he would come!"

"He has come, and I am he!" said their master. Odysseus promised to give the two men land of their own if he was victorious, and he showed them the scar on his leg to prove who he was. The farmers hugged him and shed tears of joy. Then Odysseus told them to follow him back into the hall, where he would ask for the bow. He told Eumayus to place the bow in his hands no matter what the suitors said.

When the three men returned to the hall, Antinous was trying in vain to bend the bow. Finally, he begged to put off the test until the next day. On hearing that, Odysseus asked for a chance to string the bow. The suitors told him he could not, and they threatened him.

But Penelope said the beggar could try his strength. She agreed that he was not a suitor and she could not marry him if he succeeded. But she would give him new clothes, a sword, and a spear and would send him wherever he wanted to go.

26. Why did the suitors warm and grease the bow?

    a. They were making it easier for Odysseus to string.
    b. Whoever greased it best got to marry Penelope.
    c. Greasing the bow would make it easier to bend.

27. With whom did Eumayus and the cow farmer say they would side?

    a. The suitors
    b. Odysseus
    c. Antinous

28. Which event happened last?

    a. Penelope said the beggar could try his strength.
    b. The suitors warmed and greased the bow.
    c. Odysseus asked for a chance to string the bow.

29. Why did Odysseus want Eumayus to give him the bow?

    a. He was going to kill the suitors with it.
    b. He wanted to help Antinous.
    c. He knew he could string it.

30. Why did Penelope say she would give the beggar clothes, a sword, and a spear if he could string the bow?

    a. He had only his beggar's clothing.
    b. He wasn't a suitor and thus couldn't marry her.
    c. Clothes, a sword, and a spear were prizes for stringing the bow.

31. How did Eumayus feel toward Odysseus?

    a. Loyal
    b. Jealous
    c. Embarrassed

Lessons 21–30

32. Here's a fact: *The man had a bad sunburn.*
    Which one of the following items is relevant to the fact?

    a. The man was wearing a red shirt.
    b. The man had spent the day on the beach.
    c. The man had been playing with matches.

33. Here's a fact: *The dog was panting loudly.*
    Which one of the following items is irrelevant to the fact?

    a. The dog had been running.
    b. It was very hot outside.
    c. The dog was a poodle.

Read the facts below. Then answer items 34 and 35.

Fact A: Lila is wearing an apron.
Fact B: Lila is doing her homework.

34. Which one of the following statements is relevant to fact A?

    a. She lives in Ames, Iowa.
    b. She is making cookies.
    c. Her favorite subject is math.

35. Which one of the following statements is relevant to fact B?

    a. She is using a calculator.
    b. She plans to be a chef.
    c. She has brown hair and blue eyes.

36. What do you call a young person who learns a craft from an older person?

    a. A minstrel
    b. An apprentice
    c. A saddle maker

37. Why did the length of the apprenticeship depend on the craft?

    a. Some of the masters just wanted the apprentices to run errands.
    b. The apprentices liked living at their masters' homes.
    c. Some crafts were more difficult to learn.

38. How did Mr. Warfield know the Dunns were growing a garden?

    a. Mrs. Callahan told him.
    b. Water from Mrs. Dunn's watering can splashed on his head.
    c. He saw the garden in a dream.

39. Which character claims to be "a reasonable person"?

    a. Mrs. Dunn
    b. Mrs. Grotowski
    c. Mr. Warfield

40. Why did Mr. Warfield agree to let the Dunns keep the garden?

    a. Mrs. Dunn let Mr. Warfield think it was his idea.
    b. Mrs. Dunn threatened Mr. Warfield.
    c. Mr. Dunn begged Mr. Warfield.

41. What would you find in an artists' colony?

    a. Many artists
    b. Ants
    c. Pilgrims

42. In "The Last Leaf," what is meant by the statement "Pneumonia was not a well-mannered stranger"?

    a. The doctor had never seen pneumonia.
    b. A person can get pneumonia from falling leaves.
    c. It was a serious disease and came with no warning.

Read the passage below. Then answer items 43–48.

The third son apprenticed himself to a turner. Because turning is a difficult trade, it took him a long time to learn it. One day, he received a letter from his brothers with all their bad news. They explained how the innkeeper had stolen their treasures on the last night of their travels.

Finally, the young turner had learned his trade and was ready to travel around the world. To reward the apprentice for his good conduct, the master gave him a sack and told him there was a stick inside it.

"The sack may be useful to me," said the new journeyman. "But what is the good of the stick?"

"I will tell you," answered the master. "If anyone does you any harm, just say 'Stick, out of the sack!' Then the stick will jump out upon them and beat them so soundly that they will not be able to move for a week. It will not stop until you say, 'Stick, into the sack!' "

The journeyman thanked the master, took up the sack, and started on his travels. When anyone attacked him, he would say, "Stick, out of the sack!" Then the stick would immediately jump out and deal a shower of blows on the attacker, quickly ending the affair.

One evening, the young turner reached the inn where his two brothers had been fooled. He laid his sack on the table and began to describe all the wonderful things he had seen in the world.

"Yes," he said loudly, "you may talk of self-covering tables, gold-spitting donkeys, and so forth. These are good things, but they are nothing in comparison with the treasure I carry with me in my sack!"

Then the innkeeper opened his ears.

"What in the world can it be?" he thought. "Very likely the sack is full of precious stones. I have a perfect right to it, for all good things come in threes."

43. Why did the third son stay at the inn where his brothers had stayed?

   a. He had heard the food was good there.
   b. He wanted to teach the innkeeper a lesson.
   c. The stick told him to stay there.

44. What will the innkeeper probably do?

   a. Attack the third son
   b. Write a letter apologizing to the other two brothers
   c. Steal the sack

45. What did the innkeeper mean when he said all good things come in threes?

   a. Because he had the treasures of the other two brothers, he thought he should have the third son's treasure as well.
   b. It was the third day of the month.
   c. He also had three sons.

46. What will probably happen if the innkeeper tries to steal the sack?

   a. The sack will turn to gold.
   b. The young turner will say, "Stick, out of the sack," and the stick will beat the innkeeper.
   c. The young turner will write a letter to his brothers about the theft.

47. What will the young turner do after that?

   a. Return to his master for another sack
   b. Find his brothers' treasures and go home
   c. Warn other travelers about the dishonest innkeeper

48. Why did the innkeeper think the sack probably held precious stones?

   a. Because the third son was a rich turner
   b. Because the sack was very heavy
   c. Because the other two brothers had valuable treasures

STOP - end of test - SCORE: _____

Lesson 40

For items 1–6, circle the letter of the answer that means the same thing as the underlined part.

1. We felt sad and lonely when our favorite teacher retired.

   a. exquisite
   b. forlorn
   c. distinguished

2. The detective tried to find a reason for the crime.

   a. twitch
   b. plume
   c. motive

3. The girl threw away the broken cup.

   a. detained
   b. discarded
   c. summoned

4. The small but triumphant army marched proudly into the city.

   a. victorious
   b. defeated
   c. wretched

5. Did you behold the beautiful sunset?

   a. photograph
   b. observe
   c. draw

6. Mrs. Hagashi suddenly recollected where her keys were.

   a. gathered
   b. remembered
   c. remained

For items 7–17, circle the letter of the correct answer.

7. How is Demeter different from Hades?

   a. Demeter is Greek.
   b. Demeter helps plants grow.
   c. Demeter is related to Zeus.

8. Who was Demeter's daughter?

   a. Olympus
   b. Cerberus
   c. Persephone

9. Why couldn't the sea nymphs go onto dry land?

   a. They would dry up.
   b. They had no clothing.
   c. They didn't want to be eaten by wolves.

10. Where did Hades come from?

    a. Mount Olympus
    b. The bottomless hole
    c. The sea

11. Here's a main idea from the story of Persephone: *Demeter prevented the plants from growing.*
    What is one supporting detail for that main idea?

    a. Demeter carried a torch.
    b. The earth turned brown.
    c. Demeter met with Hecate.

Read the passage below. Then answer items 12–17.

Sara was a pupil at Miss Minchin's boarding school. One day, Sara found out that her father had died. Miss Minchin called Sara into the parlor and said, "Everything will be different now. I sent for you to talk to you and make you understand. Your father is dead. You have no friends. You have no money. You have no home and no one to take care of you."

Sara's pale little face twitched nervously, but her green-gray eyes did not move from Miss Minchin's—and still Sara said nothing.

"What are you staring at?" demanded Miss Minchin sharply. "Are you so stupid that you don't understand what I mean? I tell you that you are quite alone in the world and have no one to do anything for you, unless I choose to keep you here."

Miss Minchin could not bear to find herself with a little beggar on her hands.

"Now listen to me," she went on, "and remember what I say. If you work hard and make yourself useful, I shall let you stay here. You are only a child, but you are a very sharp child, and you learn things almost without being taught. You speak French very well, and in a year or so, you can begin to help with the younger pupils. By the time you are fifteen, you ought to be able to do that much at least."

Miss Minchin was a clever business woman. She knew that this determined child could be very useful to her and save her the trouble of paying large salaries to French teachers.

12. Why was Miss Minchin so angry with Sara?

   a. Sara was rude to her.
   b. Sara did not have any money.
   c. Sara did not want to teach French.

13. What problem would Miss Minchin solve by having Sara teach French?

   a. She could help Sara improve her French.
   b. She would not have to pay a French teacher.
   c. She could help Sara earn money.

14. What would Miss Minchin probably do if Sara had a lot of money?

   a. Send Sara to another school
   b. Keep Sara as a pupil
   c. Help Sara earn more money

15. Why didn't any of Sara's relatives come to help her?

   a. Her relatives trusted Miss Minchin.
   b. Her relatives lived far away.
   c. She had no one to take care of her.

16. After Sara's father died, why did Miss Minchin decide to keep Sara at the school?

   a. Sara could teach Greek.
   b. Sara's father had given her money.
   c. Sara could be useful to her.

17. Which character was clever at business?

   a. Sara
   b. Sara's father
   c. Miss Minchin

STOP - end of test - SCORE: _____

Lesson 50

Name _____

For items 1–6, circle the letter of the answer that means the same thing as the underlined part.

1. The expensive hotel was <u>elegant</u> in every way.

   a. luxurious
   b. bedraggled
   c. drab

2. The wise woman <u>thought about</u> the meaning of life.

   a. pondered
   b. caressed
   c. jostled

3. The <u>very faithful</u> hound waited for its master.

   a. vague
   b. impudent
   c. devoted

4. The man <u>shuffled</u> carrying the heavy load.

   a. skipped happily
   b. walked slowly
   c. jumped high

5. Did you <u>vent your anger</u> when you got into the accident?

   a. hide your anger
   b. call the police
   c. let your anger show

6. Mom received a <u>parcel</u> on her birthday.

   a. summons
   b. telegram
   c. package

For items 7–17, circle the letter of the correct answer.

7. Here's a simile: *In summer, the city was like an oven.*
   What does that simile mean?

   a. The city was made of metal.
   b. The city had a door.
   c. The city was very hot.

8. Here's an exaggeration: *The baseball player hit the ball a mile.*
   What did the baseball player really do?

   a. Hit the ball one mile away
   b. Hit the ball ten feet away
   c. Hit the ball a long way

9. Here's a metaphor: *The dancer was a swan in flight.*
   To what is the dancer being compared?

   a. A plane
   b. A bird
   c. A sled

10. Here's a statement. *The con man was a sly fox.*
    What type of figurative language does that statement use?

    a. Simile
    b. Metaphor
    c. Exaggeration

11. Here's a statement. *I'm so tired I could sleep for a year.*
    What type of figurative language does that statement use?

    a. Simile
    b. Metaphor
    c. Exaggeration

Read the passage below. Then answer items 12–17.

A few nights later, a very odd thing happened. Sara found something in the room that she certainly would never have expected. When she came in as usual, she saw something small and dark in her chair—an odd, tiny figure, which turned a small and weird-looking face toward her.

"Why, it's the monkey!" Sara cried. "It is the Indian Gentleman's monkey!"

It was the monkey, sitting up and looking forlorn. Very soon, Sara found out how he had gotten into her room. The skylight was open, and it was easy to guess that he had crept out of his master's garret window, which was only a few feet away. The monkey had probably been attracted by the light in Sara's attic and had crept in. And there he was.

When Sara went up to the monkey, he actually put out his elfish little hands, caught her dress, and jumped into her arms.

"Oh, you poor little thing!" said Sara, caressing him. "I can't help liking you, but you have such a forlorn look on your little face."

The monkey sat and looked at Sara while she talked. He seemed much interested in her remarks, judging by his eyes and his forehead and the way he moved his head up and down. He examined her quite seriously. He felt the material of her dress, touched her hands, climbed up and examined her ears, and then sat on her shoulder holding a lock of her hair, looking mournful but not at all agitated. Upon the whole, the monkey seemed pleased with Sara.

"I must take you back," she said to the monkey, "though I'm sorry to have to do it. Oh, you would be good company!"

12. What is the main idea of the passage?

   a. The monkey's master had garret windows.
   b. A friendly little monkey came into Sara's room.
   c. The monkey held a lock of Sara's hair.

13. What is one supporting detail for that main idea?

   a. The monkey jumped into Sara's arms.
   b. Sara lived in London.
   c. Sara was a student of Miss Minchin's.

14. What is the most likely reason the monkey looked forlorn?

   a. He wanted to go back to his master.
   b. Sara said his face was weird looking.
   c. He didn't like the light in the attic.

15. How did the monkey examine Sara?

   a. Roughly
   b. Lightly
   c. Seriously

16. What is the last thing Sara did?

   a. Went up to the monkey
   b. Saw something in her chair
   c. Talked to the monkey

17. Why did Sara keep talking to the monkey?

   a. He looked mournful.
   b. She wanted to talk him into staying with her.
   c. He seemed to understand what she was saying.

STOP - end of test - SCORE: _____

Lesson 60

For items 1–12, circle the letter of the answer that means the same thing as the underlined part.

1. My grandmother was <u>weak and delicate</u> for a few weeks after her illness.

   a. decked out
   b. obliged
   c. frail

2. Our group came up with a great <u>plan</u> for our project.

   a. proposal
   b. incident
   c. miscalculation

3. It was difficult for Karl to <u>tolerate</u> the long and boring speech.

   a. endure
   b. maneuver
   c. spurn

4. We had a nice dinner at the <u>party after the wedding</u>.

   a. reception
   b. parasol
   c. hostler

5. Did someone <u>tell</u> the ending of the mystery?

   a. efface
   b. reveal
   c. croon

6. Mom's old and <u>hard-to-find</u> silver pattern might be in antique stores.

   a. rare
   b. humiliating
   c. gallant

7. The tragic movie was full of <u>melancholy</u> characters.

   a. violent
   b. sarcastic
   c. sad

8. That <u>absurd</u> ending just cannot be true.

   a. ridiculous
   b. nonfiction
   c. serious

9. The bird sat on the largest <u>bough</u> of the apple tree.

   a. branch
   b. leaf
   c. fruit

10. The <u>slender</u> boy was able to squeeze under the fence.

    a. chubby
    b. tall
    c. slim

11. I wonder what is at the <u>core</u> of the earth.

    a. edge
    b. apple
    c. center

12. He will call you <u>anon</u> in an hour.

    a. again
    b. tomorrow
    c. as soon as possible

For items 13–53, circle the letter of the correct answer.

Lessons 31–40

13. Which character was a three-headed monster?

   a. Hades
   b. Cerberus
   c. Zeus

14. How was the food that Persephone was used to different from Hades' food?

   a. She enjoyed fresh fruit and bread.
   b. She did not like any foods.
   c. She liked richer foods.

15. What did seeing the magnificent flower make Demeter think?

   a. That Persophone had begun gardening
   b. That the sea nymphs had left the water
   c. That Persephone was in trouble

16. Here's a fact: *My aunt wrote her autobiography last year.*
   Which one of the following items is relevant to the fact?

   a. My aunt's name is Sally.
   b. My aunt has had an interesting life.
   c. We visited my aunt in Boston.

17. Here's a fact: *Chad won the 100-yard dash.*
   Which one of the following items is irrelevant to the fact?

   a. Chad has been practicing for months.
   b. Chad is a sophomore this year.
   c. Chad finished far ahead of the other runners.

18. Here's a main idea from *Sara Crewe: Sara's life changed entirely after she moved into the attic.*
   What is one supporting detail for that main idea?

   a. Nobody noticed her except to order her around.
   b. She had a doll named Emily.
   c. The other students were rich.

Read the passage below. Then answer items 19–24.

Our story must now move out of Hades' dominions to observe what Demeter has been doing since her daughter was kidnapped. You will remember that we had a glimpse of her, half-hidden among the waving grain, while Persephone went swiftly whirling by in Hades' chariot. You will remember, too, the loud scream Persephone gave just when the chariot was out of sight.

Of all Persephone's outcries, this last shriek was the only one that reached Demeter's ears. She had mistaken the rumbling of the chariot wheels for a peal of thunder. She imagined a rain shower was coming and that it would help her make the corn grow.

At the sound of Persephone's shriek, Demeter looked about in every direction. She did not know where the shriek had come from, but she felt almost certain it was her daughter's voice.

It seemed unlikely that Persephone should have strayed over so many lands and seas. Nevertheless, Demeter decided to go home and assure herself that her daughter was safe.

Knowing that Persephone might be at the seashore, she hastened there as fast as she could. She soon beheld the wet faces of the poor sea nymphs peeping over a wave. These good creatures had been waiting on the sponge bank. Every minute or so, they popped their heads above water to see if Persephone had come back.

19. What did Demeter think the rumbling of the chariot wheels was?

   a. A rain shower
   b. A peal of thunder
   c. Persephone's shriek

20. Why did Demeter decide to go home?

   a. She was finished working in the field.
   b. She wanted to assure herself that Persephone was safe.
   c. She knew Persephone had been kidnapped.

Name _____

21. Why did Demeter hurry to the seashore?

   a. She wanted to find out if Persephone was there.
   b. She didn't want Persephone to play with the nymphs.
   c. She needed to get back to her fields.

22. In which place would you find sand and shells?

   a. In Hades' chariot
   b. In Demeter's cornfield
   c. At the seashore

23. Why didn't Demeter follow the chariot?

   a. She didn't see where the chariot went.
   b. She knew Persephone wasn't in the chariot.
   c. She decided to keep working in the field.

24. What will Demeter probably do next?

   a. Make necklaces for the nymphs
   b. Show the nymphs how the shriek sounded
   c. Ask the sea nymphs if they've seen Persephone

Lessons 41–50

25. What creature did Sara and Erma feed from the garret window?

   a. A sparrow
   b. Melvin
   c. The monkey

26. Why did Sara give the beggar girl some buns from the bakery?

   a. The girl said she would repay Sara.
   b. Sara knew what it was like to be hungry.
   c. The bakery owner told her to.

27. Here is some evidence: *Some flowers have large, colorful petals. An orchid is a flower.* So what do you know about orchids?

   a. Maybe orchids have large, colorful petals.
   b. Orchids have large, colorful petals.
   c. Orchids don't have large, colorful petals.

28. Here's a statement: *I'm so hungry I could eat a horse.* What type of figurative language does that statement use?

   a. Exaggeration
   b. Metaphor
   c. Simile

29. Here's a statement: *Brent always runs the fifty-yard dash.* Which one of the following items contradicts the statement?

   a. In his last race, Brent ran more than a mile.
   b. Brent practices running from our house to the corner.
   c. Brent's race was over in seconds.

30. Here is a statement. *I have never traveled outside the United States.* Which one of the following items contradicts the statement?

   a. I had my picture taken beside the Eiffel Tower in Paris.
   b. Last summer, we vacationed in Oregon.
   c. The Grand Canyon is my favorite place.

Read the passage below. Then answer items 31–36.

He was really a very nice rat and did not mean the least harm. When he had stood on his hind legs and sniffed the air, with his bright eyes fixed on Sara, he had hoped she would understand this. When something inside him told him that Sara would not hurt him, he went softly toward the crumbs and began to eat them. As he ate, he glanced every now and then at Sara, just as the sparrows had done, and his expression touched her heart.

Sara sat and watched him without making any movement. One crumb was much larger than the others—in fact, it could scarcely be called a crumb. The rat wanted that piece very much, but it lay quite near the footstool, and he was still rather timid.

"I believe he wants it to carry to his family in the wall," Sara thought. "If I do not stir at all, perhaps he will come and get it."

90   Reading Mastery Plus, Level 6

Sara scarcely allowed herself to breathe, she was so deeply interested. The rat shuffled a little nearer and ate a few more crumbs; then he stopped and sniffed delicately. He gave a side glance at Sara and darted at the piece of bun just as the sparrow had earlier. The instant he had the bun, he fled back to the wall, slipped down a crack, and was gone.

31. What was the rat eating in Sara's room?

a. Crumbs from Sara's toast
b. Cookie crumbs
c. Crumbs from a bun

32. Which one of the following events occurred last?

a. The rat ate the crumbs.
b. The rat fled through a crack in the wall.
c. Sara sat without moving, watching the rat.

33. Why did the rat hesitate to come close to Sara?

a. He was afraid she would hurt him.
b. He had heard she was dangerous.
c. He was afraid she had poisoned the crumbs.

34. What is the main idea of the passage?

a. Sara thought the rat looked like a sparrow.
b. The rat learned to trust Sara.
c. Rats have a well-developed sense of smell.

35. What is one supporting idea for that main idea?

a. Something inside the rat told him that Sara was a safe person.
b. The rat sniffed delicately.
c. Sara liked the rat's expression.

36. What will the rat probably do next?

a. Try to get to the kitchen for larger crumbs
b. Stay away from Sara's room
c. Come back to Sara's room for more food

Lessons 51–60

37. Here is a statement from "The Tide Rises, the Tide Falls": *The little waves, with their soft white hands, efface the footprints in the sands.* To what are the waves being compared?

a. Clocks
b. People
c. Seaweed

38. In "The Necklace," how was Matilda different from her husband?

a. She was very poor.
b. She worked in a government office.
c. She was not satisfied with what they had.

39. What is one thing Matilda probably did *not* learn from her experience?

a. All diamonds are real.
b. Be satisfied with what you have.
c. Always tell the truth.

40. What color was the dress Miss Terwilliger wore to social functions?

a. Shell pink
b. Multicolored
c. Robin's-egg blue

41. Which character mixes up his or her words?

a. The sheriff
b. Uncle Telly
c. Miss Terwilliger

42. In "A White Heron," what was the main decision Sylvia had to make?

a. Whether to stay with Mrs. Tilley
b. How to spend the hundred dollars
c. Whether to tell the hunter where the heron was

43. Why had Mrs. Tilley taken Sylvia in?

a. She was paid a hundred dollars.
b. Sylvia kept her from being lonely.
c. She wanted a servant girl.

44. Here is one main idea from "A White Heron":
The young man has a collection of stuffed birds.
What is one supporting detail for that main idea?

    a. The only bird he wants is the white heron.
    b. He is nice to young girls.
    c. He has dozens of preserved birds.

45. Here's a statement from "Written in March":
Like an army defeated the snow hath retreated.
What type of figurative language does that statement use?

    a. Exaggeration
    b. Simile
    c. Metaphor

46. Here is some evidence: *Some boys with red hair are named Andrew. Andrew is a boy.*
So what do you know about Andrew?

    a. Andrew has red hair.
    b. Andrew might have red hair.
    c. Andrew doesn't have red hair.

47. How did you figure out the answer to item 46?

    a. By making a deduction
    b. By using words from the statement
    c. By looking in the answer key

Read the passage below. Then answer items 48–53.

One Sunday, Matilda took a walk to refresh herself from a hard week's work. She suddenly saw a woman leading a child. It was Mrs. Forester. She still looked young and beautiful and charming.

Matilda felt moved. Should she speak to Mrs. Forester? Yes, certainly. Now that Matilda had paid for the necklace, she would tell Mrs. Forester all about it. Why not?

She went up to her former friend.

"Hello, Mrs. Forester," she said.

Mrs. Forester did not recognize Matilda at all and stammered, "But . . . Madame . . . I do not know . . . you must be mistaken."

"No. I am Matilda Loisel."

Matilda's friend uttered a cry.

"Oh, my poor Matilda! You have changed so much!"

"Yes, I have had many hard days since I last saw you—and all because of you!"

"Of me! How so?"

"Do you remember that diamond necklace you loaned me to wear at the ball?"

"Yes. Well?"

"Well, I lost it."

"What do you mean? You brought it back."

"I brought you another one just like it. And we have been paying for it for ten years. It was not easy for us, because we had nothing. But at last it is over, and I am very glad."

Mrs. Forester's face seemed frozen.

"You say you purchased a necklace of diamonds to replace mine?"

"Yes. You never noticed it, then. They were very much alike."

And Matilda smiled with joy.

Mrs. Forester was deeply moved, and she took Matilda's two hands.

"Oh, my poor Matilda! Why, my necklace was fake! It was worth less than five hundred francs!"

48. Why did Mrs. Forester's face seem frozen?

    a. She was frightened by what Matilda told her.
    b. She realized that Matilda had made a terrible mistake.
    c. She felt very cold toward Matilda.

49. How did you figure out the answer to item 48?

    a. By making a deduction
    b. By using words from the passage
    c. By looking in the answer key

50. What will Mrs. Forester probably do next?

    a. Give Matilda the necklace
    b. Put the necklace in a safe
    c. Give Matilda five hundred francs

51. What mistake had Matilda made about the necklace she borrowed?

    a. She believed that it was made of real diamonds.
    b. She believed that it was a copy.
    c. She believed that it was beautiful.

52. Why did Matilda have to work so hard?

    a. She wanted to keep busy.
    b. She had to help pay for the necklace.
    c. Her husband was dead.

53. At first, why did Mrs. Forester say that she didn't know Matilda?

    a. She was embarrassed by Matilda.
    b. Matilda had changed so much.
    c. She wanted to keep the necklace.

STOP - end of test - SCORE: _____

Lesson 70

For items 1–8, circle the letter of the answer that means the same thing as the underlined part.

1. The <u>small and weak</u> boy was no match for the bully.

    a. untidy
    b. puny
    c. muffled

2. The colonies <u>resisted</u> the authority of England.

    a. rebelled against
    b. sicced
    c. marred

3. A person with a lot of energy and ambition has <u>spirit</u>.

    a. loot
    b. bait
    c. spunk

4. The <u>rough</u> weather made it difficult for the sailors.

    a. naval
    b. harsh
    c. strained

5. Phil smiled at Rachel after she <u>hailed</u> him on the street.

    a. threw things at
    b. waved and shouted to
    c. grabbed

6. The man was so <u>stirred</u> by the music that he began to weep.

    a. moved
    b. annoyed
    c. deafened

7. The travelers visited all the <u>principal</u> places in the city.

    a. most royal
    b. most important
    c. least interesting

8. The <u>gale</u> made us fearful that a hurricane was coming.

    a. strong wind
    b. news report
    c. driving rain

For items 9–23, circle the letter of the correct answer.

9. Why did Frisco Kid keep a magazine page with a picture of a family on it?

    a. He imagined being in such a family.
    b. He wanted to visit them when he returned to shore.
    c. He wanted to get married and have a family like that someday.

10. At the beginning of *The Cruise of the Dazzler,* why was Joe proud of his new life at sea?

    a. All his friends were becoming sailors.
    b. His mother wanted him to become a sailor.
    c. He wanted to show his father that he could take care of himself.

11. In the following sentence, the star shows where a word is missing.
    *Three bottles were on the red shelf, but two * were on the floor.*
    What word is missing from the sentence?

    a. bottles
    b. shelves
    c. floors

12. In the following sentence, the star shows where a word is missing.

*In our class, fourteen students are girls, and twelve * are boys.*

What word is missing from the sentence?

a. class
b. girls
c. students

In the paragraph below, the sentences are numbered. Read the paragraph. Then answer items 13 and 14.

(1) Ivan was talking about his car. (2) "My car is fantastic," he said. (3) "The body is rusted and the tires are bald."

13. Which sentence is an example of sarcasm?

a. 1
b. 2
c. 3

14. Which sentence contradicts the sarcastic sentence?

a. 1
b. 2
c. 3

In the passage below, the sentences are numbered. Read the passage. Then answer items 15–17.

(1) "Hello, Jacob," said Ruth as she sat down next to him in the lunchroom.
(2) The boy looked at her and removed his glasses.
(3) "Aren't you talking to me?" she asked as she opened a carton of milk.
(4) "Not here. (5) It's much too crowded."
(6) "What do you mean? (7) Zelda is the only other person at this table."

15. Which character says sentence 4?

a. Jacob
b. Ruth
c. Zelda

16. Which character says sentence 6?

a. Jacob
b. Ruth
c. Zelda

17. In sentence 5, what does the word *it* refer to?

a. The school
b. The lunchroom
c. Jacob's glasses

Read the passage below. Then answer items 18–23.

Joe heard a creaking noise in the night and saw the men hoisting the huge mainsail above him. Then Bill and Nick untied the *Dazzler* from the dock. The sloop soon caught the breeze and headed out into the bay, pulling a lifeboat and the skiff. Joe heard some talking in low tones. He heard someone say something about turning off the lights and keeping a sharp lookout, but he didn't know what to make of it.

The waterfront lights of Oakland began to slip by. A gentle north wind was blowing the sloop south, and the *Dazzler* sailed noiselessly through the water.

"Where are we going?" Joe asked Nick in a friendly tone.

"Oh, we're going to take a cargo from Bill's factory," Nick replied. Then Bill laughed as if he and Nick had a private joke. Joe didn't think Bill looked like a factory owner, but he said nothing.

Joe was sent into the cabin to blow out the cabin lamp. The *Dazzler* turned around and began to move toward the shore. Everybody kept silent except for occasional questions and answers between Bill and Pete. Finally, the sails were lowered cautiously.

Pete whispered to Frisco Kid, who went forward and dropped the anchor. Nick pulled the *Dazzler*'s lifeboat and his skiff alongside the sloop. Bill and Nick got into the skiff, and Bill said, "Make sure you keep quiet."

Then Frisco Kid motioned Joe to get into the *Dazzler*'s lifeboat. "Can you row?" Frisco Kid asked. Joe nodded his head yes. "Then take these oars," Frisco Kid continued, "and don't make a racket."

Frisco Kid moved to the front of the lifeboat, and Pete got into the back. Joe noticed that ropes were wrapped around the oar blades. It was impossible for the oars to make a noise in the water.

18. What is Oakland?

    a. The name of the lifeboat
    b. The name of the north wind
    c. The name of a town

19. Which character seemed to have something to hide?

    a. Joe
    b. Nick
    c. Frisco Kid

20. What is the main idea of the passage?

    a. The men were trying to get somewhere unseen and unheard.
    b. A north wind blows a ship south.
    c. The men were stealing a lifeboat and a skiff.

21. What is one supporting detail for that main idea?

    a. They headed out into the bay, went south, then toward the shore.
    b. They turned off the lights of the *Dazzler*.
    c. Frisco Kid told Joe to row the lifeboat.

22. Which one of the following events occurred last?

    a. Joe blew out the lamp in the cabin.
    b. Joe got into the lifeboat.
    c. The mainsail was hoisted.

23. What will the men probably do next?

    a. Jump up and yell "Surprise!"
    b. Leave the *Dazzler* and row quietly in the lifeboat and the skiff.
    c. Beat the oars against the water to scare away sharks.

STOP - end of test - SCORE: _____

Lesson 80

Name _____

For items 1–8, circle the letter of the answer that means the same thing as the underlined part.

1. After several days, the climbers reached the <u>top</u> of the mountain.

   a. summit
   b. licking
   c. vengeance

2. Ted <u>really hated</u> carrots and peas.

   a. writhed
   b. snickered
   c. despised

3. His <u>greeting</u> to me was warm and sincere.

   a. reception
   b. fit
   c. vengeance

4. The cheerleader was <u>balanced</u> on her teammate's shoulders.

   a. unheeded
   b. poised
   c. scornful

5. The football team <u>forged ahead</u> when they got the ball.

   a. went the wrong direction
   b. moved forward powerfully
   c. eased toward the goal slowly and cautiously

6. Her voice teacher said she <u>shows promise</u> to be a singer.

   a. doesn't really want
   b. vows
   c. shows talent to learn

7. We toured a <u>plantation</u> where cotton is grown.

   a. large farm
   b. greenhouse
   c. plowed field

8. The <u>ruts</u> in the road made our trip bumpy.

   a. rocks
   b. grooves
   c. painted lines

For items 9–24, circle the letter of the correct answer.

9. Here's a sentence that combines two short sentences: *That watch is made with platinum, an expensive metal.*
   The first short sentence is *That watch is made with platinum.*
   What is the second short sentence?

   a. That watch is an expensive metal.
   b. That watch is expensive.
   c. Platinum is an expensive metal.

10. Here's a fact: *The car screeched to a halt.*
    Which one of the following items is relevant to the fact?

    a. The driver saw a dog running across the road.
    b. The car was red and had whitewall tires.
    c. The driver was listening to rock music.

11. Here's an exaggeration from "Casey at the Bat": *And then when Cooney died at first, and Barrows did the same. . . ."*
    What did Cooney and Barrows actually do?

    a. Passed away on first base
    b. Got thrown out at first base
    c. Got hit hard with a ball at first base

12. Here's one main idea from the Harriet Tubman biography: *At the beginning of the story, Jim was a slave.*
    What is one supporting detail for that main idea?

    a. He went to a train station.
    b. He lived on a plantation.
    c. He moved to Canada.

13. Which of the following states was a slave state?

    a. Maryland
    b. New York
    c. Pennsylvania

14. What was the trail of hiding places called that led runaway slaves to the North?

    a. The Trail of Tears
    b. The Northern Connection
    c. The Underground Railroad

15. Why was there a reward for Harriet Tubman's capture?

    a. She knew how to read, and slaves weren't allowed to learn to read.
    b. She helped runaway slaves.
    c. She had sleeping fits, and people thought they were contagious.

Read the paragraph below. Then answer items 16–18.

By the time the ferry reached the shore, the people had become like wild animals. They poured off the ferry and ran toward the police station. The police shot into the crowd. Two men were wounded, but the mob continued with more determination than ever.

16. What is the main idea of the paragraph?

    a. The people traveled on a ferry to the police station.
    b. The police had guns.
    c. The people on the ferry were angry.

17. How did you figure out the answer to item 16?

    a. By making a deduction
    b. By looking in the answer key
    c. By using words from the passage

18. Which one of the following events occurred first?

    a. The people ran toward the police station.
    b. The ferry arrived at the dock.
    c. The police shot two men.

Read the passage below. Then answer items 19–24.

Frisco Kid, Pete, and Joe clung to the *Dazzler,* which was in danger of sinking at any moment. Meanwhile, Nelson turned the *Reindeer* around and came back toward the *Dazzler.*

"Ze wild man! Ze wild man!" Pete shrieked, watching the *Reindeer* in amazement. "He wants us to jump on his sloop. He thinks he can turn around in this gale! He will die! We will all die! Oh, ze fool! Ze fool!"

But Nelson tried the impossible. At the right moment, he turned the *Reindeer* around and hauled back toward the *Dazzler.*

"Here she comes! Get ready to jump!" Pete cried. But Frisco Kid and Joe only looked at each other. They said nothing, but they both sensed that they should stay with the *Dazzler* and rescue the safe.

The *Reindeer* dashed by them again. She was so close that it appeared she would run them down. Pete was the only one to jump. He sprang for the *Reindeer* like a cat and caught onto the railing with both hands. Then the *Reindeer* forged ahead. Pete clung to the railing and worked his way up until he dropped onto the deck.

And then, to Joe's amazement, the *Reindeer* turned around again. She plowed back toward the *Dazzler* at breakneck speed. She was tilted at such an angle that it seemed she would sink.

Just then, the storm burst in fury, and the shouting wind made the sea churn. The *Reindeer* dipped from view behind an immense wave. The wave rolled on, but the boys could see only the angry waters where the *Reindeer* had been. They looked a second time. There was no *Reindeer.* They were alone on the ocean.

19. Why was Joe so amazed when the *Reindeer* turned around for the last time?

    a. The men were trying to sink the *Dazzler.*
    b. The men were trying to save his life.
    c. The storm was the worst he had ever experienced.

20. What happened to the *Reindeer* at the end of the passage?

    a. The wave carried her far away from the *Dazzler*.
    b. She sank to the bottom of the ocean.
    c. She tipped over on her side.

21. Why did Joe stay on board the *Dazzler*?

    a. He was afraid to jump onto the *Reindeer*.
    b. He wanted to rescue the safe.
    c. He knew the *Reindeer* would sink.

22. What will Joe and Frisco Kid probably do next?

    a. Jump overboard and swim for shore
    b. Try to find the *Reindeer*
    c. Try to fix the *Dazzler*

23. How was Joe different from Pete?

    a. Joe thought the safe was important.
    b. Joe was in great danger.
    c. Joe was on board the *Dazzler*.

24. One sentence says ". . . the shouting wind made the sea churn."
    What type of figurative language does that sentence use?

    a. Simile
    b. Metaphor
    c. Exaggeration

STOP - end of test - SCORE: _____

Lesson 90

Name _____

For items 1–12, circle the letter of the answer that means the same thing as the underlined part.

1. The sailors went below to the cabin where they slept for the night.

    a. quarantine station
    b. skiff
    c. forecastle

2. Did the two cars run into each other in the intersection?

    a. collide
    b. churn
    c. hurtle

3. The quarterback used trickery to fool the other team into thinking he was going left.

    a. junction
    b. deception
    c. agony

4. Carrying the large and heavy sofa was difficult.

    a. supernatural
    b. plush
    c. bulky

5. We enjoyed the old story about Johnny Appleseed.

    a. sensation
    b. legend
    c. exception

6. Please meet me before class so we can study for the test.

    a. beforehand
    b. systematically
    c. dryly

7. She defied her sergeant's orders to run laps.

    a. waited for
    b. applauded
    c. challenged

8. She gave me a smirk when she won the bet.

    a. mocking smile
    b. handshake
    c. five-dollar bill

9. Ferdinand walked down the long hotel corridor looking for the door to his room.

    a. lobby
    b. hallway
    c. parking lot

10. Sophia is in debt after buying a car.

    a. owes money
    b. is having a great time
    c. is entering car races

11. Our grandfathers were in the same regiment in the Korean War.

    a. boot camp
    b. airplane
    c. army unit

12. I was dumbfounded when I won the prize.

    a. briefly astonished
    b. lightheaded
    c. in a coma

For items 13–53, circle the letter of the correct answer.

Lessons 61–70

13. If you want to find out where Henry Ford was born, which reference book would you use?

    a. Atlas
    b. Encyclopedia
    c. Dictionary

14. Here's a statement: *The waves were like soldiers marching.*
    What type of figurative language does that statement use?

    a. Metaphor
    b. Simile
    c. Exaggeration

15. Here's a statement: *You really did a great job of doing the dishes. There's water all over the floor. The countertops are greasy. This bowl still has cereal stuck to it.*
    What type of figurative language does that statement use?

    a. Metaphor
    b. Exaggeration
    c. Sarcasm

16. Here's a statement: *The daffodils danced in the breeze.*
    What type of figurative language does that statement use?

    a. Metaphor
    b. Exaggeration
    c. Sarcasm

Look at the map below. Then answer items 17–19.

17. In which state is St. Louis?

    a. Arkansas
    b. Iowa
    c. Missouri

18. Which city borders on the Gulf of Mexico?

    a. Minneapolis
    b. New Orleans
    c. Memphis

19. Which one of the following statements contradicts the map?

    a. Memphis is north of New Orleans.
    b. Iowa is south of Missouri.
    c. New Orleans is south of Arkansas.

Read the passage below. Then answer items 20–24.

Joe dashed out into the water for the lifeboat. Pete and Frisco Kid had the boat's nose pointed out to sea and were calmly awaiting Joe's arrival. They had their oars all ready for the start, but they held them quietly at rest. The other skiff was still on the beach. Bill was trying to shove it off and was calling on Nick to lend a hand. But Nick had lost his head completely and came floundering through the water toward the lifeboat.

Joe climbed into the heavily loaded lifeboat, and Nick followed him. Nick's extra weight nearly sank the lifeboat. In the meantime, the two men on the beach had pulled out pistols and opened fire. The alarm had spread. Voices and cries could be heard from the ships on the pier. In the distance, a police siren blew frantically.

"Get out!" Frisco Kid shouted at Nick. "You ain't going to sink us. Go and help your partner!"

But Nick's teeth were chattering with fright, and he did not move or speak.

"Throw the crazy man out!" Pete ordered. At this moment, a bullet shattered Pete's oar, and he coolly proceeded to look for a spare one.

"Give us a hand, Joe," Frisco Kid commanded.

Joe understood, and together they seized Nick and flung him overboard. Two or three bullets splashed about him as he came to the surface just in time to be picked up by Bill, who had at last succeeded in getting the skiff into the water. A few oar strokes into the darkness quickly took them out of range of the pistols.

20. Into which boat did Nick climb?

   a. The *Dazzler*
   b. The lifeboat
   c. The skiff

21. Which man did Pete order the boys to throw out?

   a. Joe
   b. Bill
   c. Nick

22. Which character was panicking?

   a. Pete
   b. Nick
   c. Frisco Kid

23. Why were the police shooting at the boats?

   a. They were target shooting, and the boats were the targets.
   b. They were trying to scare away the men.
   c. They didn't want the men to escape.

24. In the sentence in the last paragraph that begins "Two or three bullets splashed about him as he came to the surface . . . ," to which person does *him* refer?

   a. Frisco Kid
   b. Joe
   c. Nick

Lessons 71–80

25. In the Harriet Tubman biography, which of the following events occurred last?

   a. Harriet pretended to read a book on the train.
   b. Jim was beaten when the horse broke its leg.
   c. The slaves hid under a pile of laundry in a wagon.

26. How was being a free man different from being a slave?

   a. There weren't any differences.
   b. A free man had food, clothing, and shelter.
   c. A free man could own property.

27. In the following sentence, the star shows where a word is missing.
   *Most students were in the classroom, but some * were on the playground.*
   What word is missing from the sentence?

   a. classrooms
   b. playgrounds
   c. students

In the passage below, the sentences are numbered. Read the passage. Then answer items 28–30.

(1) "Hi, Matt," said Emily as she came onto the tennis court.

(2) The boy was swinging his racket as if he were hitting a tennis ball.

(3) "Are you ready to play?" she asked as she laced up her shoes.

(4) "Yes. (5) I have a new racket."

(6) "It looks terrific. (7) Pam says your game is really improving."

28. Which character says sentence 5?

   a. Matt
   b. Emily
   c. Pam

29. Which character says sentence 6?

   a. Matt
   b. Emily
   c. Pam

30. In sentence 6, to what does the word *it* refer?

   a. The tennis court
   b. Matt's tennis racket
   c. Matt's tennis game

Read the passage below. Then answer items 31–36.

One cold night, I heard some slaves talking about a woman named Moses.

Old George said, "Moses has led so many runaways out of the South that the masters will pay to have her captured—dead or alive."

"She's eight feet tall," Old George continued in a whisper. "She can carry a grown man under each arm and still run faster than any slave catcher."

"That can't be," I said. "I don't believe there is a Moses."

"Yes, there is," Henry said. He was a new slave on the plantation.

"How do you know?" I asked.

"Moses is an old friend of mine," he said. "Her real name is Harriet Tubman. She will come for me

one of these days, and she will take any of you who are brave enough to go."

Moses was real! For the first time in my life, I believed I had a chance to be free. I had been a slave all my life, and I wanted freedom. I had heard stories about how free blacks lived in the north. A free man could own property. He could work for anyone he wanted to, and no one could treat him like an animal.

I wanted to be free, but fear kept me from running away. On the plantation, I had food every day, even if it was never enough. The master gave us clothes to wear and a cabin to sleep in.

How did a free man get food, clothing, and shelter? I did not know, and I was afraid of the unknown world outside the plantation. One thing I did know was that if I ran away and got caught, the master would beat me so hard I might die.

31. Which slaves could go north with Harriet?

   a. Any who could pay five thousand dollars
   b. Any the masters were willing to set free
   c. Any who were brave enough

32. One sentence says that Harriet is eight feet tall. What type of figurative language does that sentence use?

   a. Simile
   b. Exaggeration
   c. Metaphor

33. What kept Jim from running away?

   a. Fear of the unknown
   b. Fear of animals
   c. Fear of running

34. What does Jim not understand about freedom?

   a. Why Harriet was called Moses
   b. How free men met their physical needs
   c. Why his master would beat him

35. What will Jim probably do next?

   a. Go to the master's house for a feast
   b. Write a book about being a slave
   c. Think more about Henry's words

36. What is the main idea of the passage?

   a. Jim thought about being a free man.
   b. Harriet can run faster than the slave catchers.
   c. Slaves were treated like animals.

Lessons 81–90

37. In the Harriet Tubman biography, what was Jim's occupation as a free man?

   a. Cabinetmaker
   b. Conductor on the Underground Railroad
   c. Raiding party leader

38. Why did Jim become a soldier?

   a. He would be paid.
   b. He wanted other slaves to be free as he was.
   c. His children wanted him to.

39. In *All in Favor,* what does Nancy believe about the vote to join the club?

   a. That the vote had to be unanimous
   b. That Sidney, Harriet, and Tom had voted for her
   c. That only two votes were needed to join

40. At the end of *All in Favor,* Nancy finds out that her belief was mistaken.
   What is that an example of?

   a. Exaggeration
   b. Metaphor
   c. Irony

41. In the 1840s, what problem could electricity in a house have solved?

   a. Heating the house
   b. Earning more than a dollar a day
   c. Having to walk to school

42. How is a steamboat different from a sailboat?

   a. A steamboat doesn't need a captain.
   b. A steamboat can travel on a river.
   c. A steamboat has a shallow hull.

43. Here is one main idea from the article about life in the 1840s: *People made wild claims about pills and other medicine.*
   What is one supporting detail for that main idea?

   a. There was no cure for malaria.
   b. One ad said a potion would make you as strong as an Indian chief.
   c. Doctors were not allowed to cut up dead people.

44. Here's a fact: *My sister got a part in the play.*
   Which one of the following items is relevant to the fact?

   a. She drove my car to the audition.
   b. She says the stage had red curtains.
   c. She has been practicing for weeks.

45. Here is some evidence: *Some of Ashley's skirts are pleated. Ashley wore a skirt today.*
   So what do you know about Ashley?

   a. She wore a pleated skirt today.
   b. She might have worn a pleated skirt today.
   c. She didn't wear a pleated skirt today.

46. How did you figure out the answer to item 45?

   a. By making a deduction
   b. By combining the sentences
   c. By using words from the passage

47. Read these two sentences: *Arizona is the forty-eighth state. Arizona is known as the Grand Canyon State.*
   What is the correct way to combine the sentences?

   a. Arizona, in the Grand Canyon, is the forty-eighth state.
   b. Arizona is a state that is the forty-eighth.
   c. Arizona, the forty-eighth state, is known as the Grand Canyon State.

Read the passage below. Then answer items 48–53.

Harriet's last mission during the war was in Virginia, where she worked as a nurse until the Confederacy surrendered in 1865. The war was finally over, and the slaves were free at last. That was worth celebrating.

Harriet had worked as a soldier during the war. She had spied; she had led raiding parties; she had fought in furious battles; she had convinced slaves to leave their plantations; and she had worked as an army nurse. Her great job was completed, but her troubles were not over.

When Harriet returned to Auburn, New York, in 1865, she was treated as a hero. But she had no money. She had never been paid one cent for her efforts during the war, and she was now deep in debt.

A woman named Sarah Bradford helped Harriet earn money. Sarah helped Harriet write a book about her adventures. The book made a fair amount of money, and Sarah gave every cent to Harriet. But the government still refused to pay Harriet for her services.

A lot of people testified that Harriet deserved the money. A general from the North wrote, "She made many a raid inside the enemy lines, displaying remarkable courage." A doctor who worked in a hospital in South Carolina praised her for her "kindness and attention to the sick and suffering." Others told about the unselfish deeds Harriet had done. But the government still refused to pay her.

48. Who kept the money for the book Harriet and Sarah wrote?

    a. The government
    b. Harriet
    c. The publisher

49. Which one of the following events occurred last?

    a. Harriet worked as a nurse.
    b. The slaves were freed.
    c. The government refused to pay Harriet.

50. Why did people testify about what Harriet had done during the war?

    a. They wanted the government to pay Harriet for her services.
    b. They were writing a book about Harriet.
    c. They were trying to help Harriet get a job.

51. Why did Harriet help people during the war?

    a. She wanted someone to write a book about her someday.
    b. She was an unselfish person.
    c. She wanted to celebrate when the slaves were freed.

52. Where did Harriet live after the war ended?

    a. The South
    b. The North
    c. Canada

53. How does Harriet probably face her troubles with the government?

    a. In a kindly way
    b. Laughingly
    c. Courageously

STOP - end of test - SCORE: _____

Lesson 100

For items 1–8, circle the letter of the answer that means the same thing as the underlined part.

1. The boy was so <u>deeply involved</u> in his reading that he didn't hear the phone ring.

   a. harassed
   b. casual
   c. absorbed

2. The girl made a <u>mistake</u> on her test.

   a. scuffle
   b. sermon
   c. blunder

3. I was <u>puzzled</u> by her strange remark.

   a. perplexed
   b. considerable
   c. foolhardy

4. She <u>slept lightly</u> on the train trip.

   a. lulled
   b. dozed
   c. sidled

5. The jeweler looked closely at the diamond to see if it was <u>genuine</u>.

   a. real
   b. large
   c. red

6. The astronomer <u>contemplated</u> the vastness of space.

   a. ignored
   b. was afraid of
   c. thought about

7. The president repeated the <u>oath</u> of office as he was sworn in.

   a. solemn promise
   b. essay
   c. application

8. We walked <u>gingerly</u> on the icy street.

   a. hurriedly
   b. cautiously
   c. backward

For items 9–23, circle the letter of the correct answer.

9. Here is some evidence: *Some of my cousins live in Texas. Mike is my cousin.*
   So what do you know about Mike?

   a. Maybe he lives in Texas.
   b. He lives in Texas.
   c. He doesn't live in Texas.

10. In the following sentence, the star shows where a word is missing.
    *Five * were ill, but the other members came to the meeting at the field.*

    a. meetings
    b. members
    c. fields

11. Here's a sentence that combines two short sentences. *Tom painted the fence with whitewash, a watery white substance.*
    The first short sentence is *Tom painted the fence with whitewash.*
    What is the second short sentence?

    a. Whitewash is a watery white substance.
    b. That paint is whitewash.
    c. That paint is a white, watery substance.

12. If you want to know how to pronounce the word *cough,* which reference book would you use?

    a. Atlas
    b. Encyclopedia
    c. Dictionary

13. What problems did Aunt Polly have in disciplining Tom?

   a. He was bigger than she was.
   b. He would always run into the church.
   c. She didn't have the heart to punish him.

14. Where did Outlaw Joe kill Dr. Robinson?

   a. In the graveyard
   b. In the schoolyard
   c. Behind Tom's fence

In the paragraph below, the sentences are numbered. Read the paragraph. Then answer items 15 and 16.

(1) Ben was talking to Tom as Tom was whitewashing the fence.
(2) "But of course you'd rather work than go swimming, wouldn't you?" said Ben.
(3) When Tom ignored him, Ben said, "Oh, come on, let me whitewash a little bit. I'll be careful."

15. Which statement is a sample of sarcasm?

   a. 1
   b. 2
   c. 3

16. Which statement contradicts the sarcastic statement?

   a. 1
   b. 2
   c. 3

17. How did students do their writing assignments in the 1840s?

   a. With slates and chalk
   b. With their fingers in the air
   c. On typewriters

Read the passage below. Then answer items 18–23.

When Tom reached the little frame schoolhouse that Monday morning, he walked in briskly. He hung his hat on a peg and flung himself into his seat. The schoolmaster was dozing in front of the class in his great wooden armchair. He had been lulled to sleep by the drowsy hum of study. Tom's entrance woke him.

"Thomas Sawyer!"

Tom knew that when his name was pronounced in full, it meant trouble.

"Sir!"

"Come up here. Why are you late again, as usual?"

Tom was about to lie when he saw two long tails of yellow hair hanging down a back that he recognized. It was the Adored Unknown Girl! And next to her was the only vacant place on the girls' side of the schoolhouse.

Tom instantly said, "I STOPPED TO TALK WITH HUCKLEBERRY FINN!"

The schoolmaster's heart stopped, and he stared helplessly. The buzz of study ceased. The pupils wondered if this foolhardy boy had lost his mind. The master said:

"You . . . did what?"

"Stopped to talk with Huckleberry Finn."

There was no mistaking the words.

"Thomas Sawyer, this is the most astounding confession I have ever listened to. You will be punished for this."

Then the order followed: "Thomas Sawyer, I order you to go and sit with the girls! And let this be a warning to you."

18. Why was Tom late for school?

   a. He stopped to talk with Huck Finn.
   b. He was lulled to sleep by the hum of study.
   c. He had forgotten his books.

19. Why did Tom tell the schoolmaster the truth?

   a. He was afraid of the schoolmaster.
   b. He wanted to sit with the girls.
   c. He was not a good liar.

20. What will probably happen when Tom sits down?

    a. Tom will get the Adored Unknown Girl's attention.
    b. Tom will wave to his friends on the boys' side.
    c. Tom will keep quiet and obey the schoolmaster.

21. Why was the schoolmaster astonished by what Tom said?

    a. He was shocked that Tom knew Huck Finn.
    b. He had expected Tom to lie.
    c. He had expected Tom to keep quiet.

22. What is the main idea of the first paragraph?

    a. Tom woke the schoolmaster.
    b. Tom walked in briskly.
    c. The schoolmaster was sleeping.

23. How did you figure out the answer to item 22?

    a. By using words from the passage
    b. By looking in the answer key
    c. By making a deduction

STOP - end of test - SCORE: _____

Lesson 110

For items 1–8, circle the letter of the answer that means the same thing as the underlined part.

1. Everyone was shocked by the <u>horrible</u> accident.

   a. haggard
   b. blissful
   c. ghastly

2. The hamlet was <u>completely</u> destroyed by the violent storm.

   a. utterly
   b. confidentially
   c. randomly

3. Was there a great <u>high point</u> at the end of the story?

   a. topic
   b. climax
   c. folly

4. He <u>dug up</u> the toy from the pile of laundry.

   a. unearthed
   b. abused
   c. chartered

5. The old woman <u>reflected on</u> the events of her life.

   a. looked at
   b. rejected
   c. thought about

6. My brother <u>played hooky</u> once.

   a. didn't go to school
   b. was on the hooky team
   c. shot a bow and arrow

7. Eduardo seemed <u>jealous</u> when Paula received the prize he wanted.

   a. embarrassed
   b. happy
   c. suspicious

8. An X on the map made the location of the treasure <u>distinct</u>.

   a. easy to recognize
   b. hard to see
   c. uncertain

For items 9–24, circle the letter of the correct answer.

9. What was the gift Tom had given Becky?

   a. A piece of blue bottle glass
   b. A dead rat
   c. A brass doorknob

10. Why did Tom talk about the murder in his sleep?

    a. He was trying to scare Sid.
    b. He was dreaming about the murder.
    c. He wanted Aunt Polly to know he had seen the murder.

11. In the following sentence, the star shows where a word is missing. *Two * did not join in, but the other students had a good time riding the horses and petting the sheep.*
    What word is missing?

    a. horses
    b. sheep
    c. students

12. Here are two sentences: *William Wordsworth wrote about the beauty of nature. William Wordsworth was an important British poet.* Which is a correct way to combine those two sentences?

    a. William Wordsworth wrote about the beauty of nature, an important British poet.
    b. WilliamWordsworth wrote about important British poets.
    c. William Wordsworth, an important British poet, wrote about the beauty of nature.

13. Here's an argument: *My motorcycle has Haltem brakes, which are the best brakes money can buy. Because the brakes are so good, I'm certain that my motorcycle is the best around.*
    Which rule does the argument break?

    a. Just because you know about the whole thing doesn't mean you know about every part.
    b. Just because you know about one part doesn't mean you know about another part.
    c. Just because you know about a part doesn't mean you know about the whole thing.

14. Here's an argument: *That factory produces a lot of smoke, and the smoke makes people sick. If we don't close down that factory, everybody will get sick.*
    Which rule does the argument break?

    a. Just because two things happen around the same time doesn't mean that one thing causes the other thing.
    b. Just because two words sound the same doesn't mean they have the same meaning.
    c. Just because the writer presents some choices doesn't mean that there are no other choices.

Read the facts and instructions below. Then answer items 15 and 16.

Facts:
Your full name is Edna Ferber Millay. You live at 727 Lake Street in Boomwater, North Dakota. You have three children, whose names are Craig, Linda, and Derek.
Instructions:

- *On line 1, write your full name, last name first.*
- *On line 2, write the name of the state you live in.*

15. What will you write on line 1?

    a. Millay, Edna
    b. Millay, Edna Ferber
    c. Edna Ferber Millay

16. What will you write on line 2?

    a. Boomwater
    b. Dakota
    c. North Dakota

Look at the graph below. Then answer items 17 and 18.

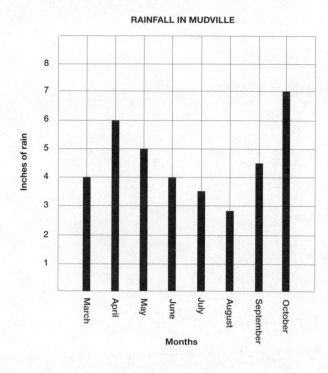

RAINFALL IN MUDVILLE

17. Which month had the least rainfall?

   a. June
   b. August
   c. October

18. Which month had seven inches of rainfall?

   a. September
   b. July
   c. October

Read the passage below. Then answer items 19–24.

A whole hour drifted by. The schoolmaster sat nodding in his chair, and the air was drowsy with the hum of study. By and by, Mr. Dobbins straightened himself, yawned, unlocked his desk, and reached for his book. But he did not know whether to take it out or leave it. Most of the pupils glanced up indifferently—but there were two that watched his movements with intent eyes.

Mr. Dobbins fingered his book absently for a while, then took it out and settled himself in his chair to read! Tom shot a glance at Becky. She looked like a hunted and helpless rabbit. Tom instantly forgot his quarrel with her. Quick—something must be done! Done in a flash, too! He had an inspiration! He would run and snatch the book, spring through the door, and run off.

But Tom waited for one little instant, and his chance was lost, for Mr. Dobbins opened the book. If Tom only had the chance back again! Too late. There was no help for Becky now, he thought. The next moment Mr. Dobbins faced his class. Every eye sank under his gaze, which even put fear in the innocent. There was silence for ten seconds while Mr. Dobbins was gathering his anger.

Then he spoke. "Who tore this book?"

There was not a sound. One could have heard a pin drop. The stillness continued. Mr. Dobbins searched face after face for signs of guilt.

19. Who tore the book?

   a. Tom
   b. Becky
   c. Mr. Dobbins

20. How did Tom feel when he looked at Becky?

   a. He felt sorry for her.
   b. He felt envy for her.
   c. He felt proud of her.

21. Why did Tom want to grab the book?

   a. He wanted to look at the pictures in the book.
   b. He didn't want Mr. Dobbins to see the torn page.
   c. He wanted to give the book to Becky.

22. What did Tom forget when he looked at Becky?

   a. His quarrel with her
   b. The name of the book
   c. His engagement to Amy Lawrence

23. One sentence says "Tom shot a glance at Becky."
What type of figurative language does that sentence use?

    a. Simile
    b. Metaphor
    c. Exaggeration

24. What will Becky probably do when Mr. Dobbins searches her face?

    a. Appear calm and innocent
    b. Say that Tom tore the book
    c. Try to cover her face

STOP - end of test - SCORE: _____

Lesson 120

For items 1–12, circle the letter of the answer that means the same thing as the underlined part.

1. The movie was about a violent train robber in the Old West.

    a. mortified
    b. vicious
    c. tranquil

2. The team was humiliated after being beaten by fifty points.

    a. crestfallen
    b. indifferent
    c. immortal

3. After many years, the dog began to look like its master.

    a. revive
    b. resemble
    c. elude

4. It was difficult climbing the steep cliff by the river.

    a. loft
    b. inlet
    c. bluff

5. The thief was a liar and a mean person.

    a. deputy
    b. sentry
    c. scoundrel

6. The visit to the war museum had a powerful effect on the students.

    a. impact
    b. relic
    c. catastrophe

7. I'd like a book for a juvenile who is fourteen.

    a. young person
    b. nonfiction
    c. reference

8. The difficult directions flustered him.

    a. confused
    b. angered
    c. worried

9. She hit her head on a stalactite.

    a. rock that forms on the floor of a cave
    b. rock that hangs from the ceiling of a cave
    c. metal supporting rod drilled into the wall of a cave

10. When I saw the hamburger, I realized how famished I was.

    a. hungry
    b. ill
    c. happy

11. The hamlet had only ten houses.

    a. short street
    b. small village
    c. road along the seacoast

12. The camp furnishes all craft materials.

    a. supplies
    b. discards
    c. chooses

For items 13–49, circle the letter of the correct answer.

Lessons 91–100

13. Who was raising Tom Sawyer?

    a. Outlaw Joe
    b. Huckleberry Finn
    c. Aunt Polly

14. What did Huck Finn say dead rats could be used for?

    a. To cure warts
    b. To attract a girl
    c. To ward off evil spirits

15. Here's a fact: *The train was late arriving in Chicago.*
    Which one of the following items is relevant to the fact?

    a. Grace travels by train every summer.
    b. The train had fourteen passenger cars.
    c. The train left New York three hours late.

In the passage below, the sentences are numbered. Read the passage. Then answer items 16–18.

    (1) Tom hailed the outcast. "Hello, Huckleberry."
    (2) "Hello, yourself."
    (3) "What's that you got?"
    (4) "Dead rat."
    (5) "Lemme see him, Huck. My, he's pretty stiff. Where'd you get him?"
    (6) "Bought him off a boy."
    (7) "What did you give?"
    (8) "I give a blue marble."
    (9) "Where'd you get the blue marble?"
    (10) "Bought it off Ben Rogers two weeks ago for a lucky rabbit's foot."

16. Which character says sentence 3?

    a. Tom
    b. Huck
    c. Ben

17. Which character says sentence 8?

    a. Tom
    b. Huck
    c. Ben

18. In sentence 6, to what does the word *him* refer?

    a. Ben
    b. Tom
    c. The dead rat

Read the passage below. Then answer items 19–24.

    About half past nine or ten o'clock, Tom returned to the deserted street to where the Adored Unknown Girl lived. He paused a moment. No sound fell upon his listening ear. A candle was casting a dull glow upon the curtain of a second-story window. Was the Adored Unknown Girl there? He climbed the fence and tiptoed through the plants until he stood under that window. He looked up at it long, and with emotion.

    Tom lay down on his back under the window. His hands were folded on his chest, holding his poor wilted flower. As he lay there, Tom imagined that he would look this way if he were dying, with no shelter over his head, no loving face to bend over him. And thus she would see him when she looked out in the morning. Would she drop one little tear upon his poor, lifeless form? Would she heave one little sigh to see a bright young life so rudely cut down?

    The window went up, a maidservant's voice broke the calm, and a torrent of water drenched poor Tom and brought him back to life. Tom sprang up with a snort, went over the fence, and shot away in the gloom.

    Later that night, Polly mentioned that Jeff Thatcher's cousin Becky had moved to Saint Petersburg. Tom said nothing.

19. What time did Tom go to Becky's house?

    a. About half past nine in the evening
    b. About half past nine in the morning
    c. About half past six in the evening

20. What is the name of the Adored Unknown Girl?

    a. Her name is not given in the passage.
    b. Polly
    c. Becky

21. Where did the maid throw the water?

    a. Into the street
    b. Over the fence
    c. Through the open window

22. What emotion was Tom feeling as he looked up at the window?

    a. Jealousy
    b. Adoration
    c. Depression

23. What will Tom probably do next?

    a. Try to see the Adored Unknown Girl again
    b. Ask Polly about the Adored Unknown Girl
    c. Throw water at the maid

24. Why did Tom say nothing at the end of the passage?

    a. He was pretending to be dead again.
    b. He was in trouble for getting home late.
    c. He didn't want anyone to know that he liked the girl.

Lessons 101–110

25. How did Aunt Polly know that Tom had been out at night?

    a. Sid was awake when Tom came home and told her.
    b. It was on the morning news.
    c. Tom's nose grew when she asked him.

26. Who told a lie about the murder to save himself?

    a. The schoolmaster
    b. Dr. Robinson
    c. Outlaw Joe

27. In the following sentence, the star shows where a word is missing.
Two dogs were on the stage when the whistle blew, but most * were still with their owners.

    a. owners
    b. stages
    c. dogs

Look at the map below. Then answer items 28–30.

28. Which city is in Missouri?

    a. Minneapolis
    b. St. Louis
    c. Memphis

29. Which one of the following states is farthest north?

    a. Iowa
    b. Arkansas
    c. Missouri

30. Which one of the following statements contradicts the map?

    a. Minneapolis is north of St. Louis.
    b. Arkansas is north of Iowa.
    c. New Orleans is south of Memphis.

Read the passage below. Then answer items 31–36.

Tom went home miserable, and his dreams that night were full of horrors. Muff Potter's trial began the next day. That day and the day after, Tom hung around the courtroom. He had a strong impulse to go in, but he forced himself to stay out.

Huck was having the same experience. The two boys carefully avoided each other. Each wandered away, from time to time, but the same dismal fascination always brought them back to the courtroom.

Tom kept his ears open when people came out of the courtroom. He always heard distressing news. It seemed that the rope was closing more and more tightly around poor Potter's neck. At the end of the second day, the gossipers said that Outlaw Joe had told his story. The evidence he gave was firm and unshaken. There was not the slightest question as to what the jury's verdict would be.

Tom was out late that night on a mission so secret that he could hardly bear to think of it. He came to bed through the window. He was in a tremendous state of excitement, and it was hours before he got to sleep.

31. Which one of the following events occurred last?

    a. Outlaw Joe tells his story in the courtroom.
    b. Tom goes to bed after being out late at night.
    c. The trial of Muff Potter begins.

32. About whom did Outlaw Joe testify?

    a. Tom
    b. Huck
    c. Muff

33. What is the main idea of the passage?

    a. Tom is confused and upset about how the trial is progressing against Muff.
    b. Tom and Huck don't want to see each other at the courthouse.
    c. Gossipers are more accurate than newspapers.

34. What is one supporting detail for that main idea?

    a. Tom likes to go out at night through the window.
    b. Tom had nightmares and was torn about seeing the trial.
    c. Tom and Huck keep having the same experiences.

35. One sentence says that the rope was closing more and more tightly around poor Potter's neck.
    What type of figurative language does that sentence use?

    a. Exaggeration
    b. Simile
    c. Metaphor

36. What will probably happen next?

    a. Tom will give evidence contradicting Outlaw Joe's story.
    b. Tom will be out late at night again.
    c. Huck and Tom will keep each other out of the courtroom.

Lessons 111–120

37. Here is one main idea from *Tom Sawyer: Tom and Becky were lost in the cave.*
    What is one supporting detail for that main idea?

    a. They were engaged to be married.
    b. They drew a picture on a slate.
    c. They went down passages at random.

38. Here's a statement: *When Tom saw Outlaw Joe, he took off at about forty miles an hour.*
    What type of figurative language does that statement use?

    a. Exaggeration
    b. Metaphor
    c. Sarcasm

39. How did Tom and Huck plan to get the box?

    a. Wait until Outlaw Joe was gone
    b. Trip Outlaw Joe and grab it
    c. Switch it with another box

40. How was the Welshman's second greeting to Huck different from the first time Huck went to his house?

    a. The second time the Welshman greeted Huck with anger.
    b. The second time the Welshman greeted Huck with indifference.
    c. The second time the Welshman greeted Huck with joy.

41. Why did the Welshman treat Huck differently the second time?

    a. Huck had told him about Outlaw Joe's plan to harm the Widow Douglas.
    b. He felt sorry because Huck had no family.
    c. His family begged him not to be rude to Huck.

42. Here is some evidence: *Some players wore cleats. Adam is a player.*
    So what do you know about Adam?

    a. He wore cleats.
    b. He didn't wear cleats.
    c. Maybe he wore cleats.

43. At the beginning of *Tom Sawyer*, what do the townspeople believe about Huck?

    a. That he is a rich person
    b. That he lives with Aunt Polly
    c. That he is a bad influence

44. At the end of *Tom Sawyer*, the townspeople find out that their belief was mistaken. What is that an example of?

    a. Irony
    b. Metaphor
    c. Exaggeration

Read the passage below. Then answer items 45–49.

Tom tried to get Becky to talk, but all her hopes were gone. Tom said the search was probably going on by now. He would shout and maybe someone would come. He tried it, but the distant echoes sounded so hideous in the darkness that he did not shout anymore.

The hours wasted away, and hunger came to torment the captives again. A portion of Tom's cake was left. They divided it and ate it, but they seemed hungrier than before.

By and by Tom said, "Sh! Did you hear that?"

Both held their breath and listened. There was a sound like the faintest, far-off shout. Instantly, Tom answered it. Leading Becky by the hand, he started groping down the corridor in its direction.

Presently he listened again. Again the sound was heard, and apparently a little nearer.

"It's them!" said Tom. "They're coming! Come along, Becky, we're all right now!"

The joy of the prisoners was almost overwhelming. Their speed was slow, however, because pitfalls were common. They shortly came to a pitfall and had to stop. It might be three feet deep, it might be a hundred—there was no passing it, at any rate. Tom got down on his chest and reached as far as he could. No bottom. They must stay there and wait until the searchers came.

As they listened, the distant shouting grew more distant. A moment or two more and it was gone altogether.

45. Which one of the following events occurred first?

    a. Tom and Becky heard far-off calling.
    b. Tom and Becky shared the last of the cake.
    c. Tom and Becky came to a pitfall in the corridor.

46. How deep was the pitfall?

    a. Three feet
    b. A hundred feet
    c. They didn't know.

47. Why did the shouting become fainter?

    a. The searchers were growing hoarse from shouting.

    b. The searchers went away.

    c. The searchers were hungry and weak.

48. What is the main idea of the passage?

    a. Tom and Becky want the searchers to find them.

    b. Tom and Becky have no more cake and are hungry.

    c. Tom and Becky are prisoners in a pit.

49. How did you figure out the answer to item 48?

    a. By subtracting 3 from 100

    b. By making a deduction

    c. By reading the beginning and end of the passage

STOP - end of test - SCORE: _____

Pretend you live in the 1930s and are looking for a job. You want to advertise your services on a sandwich board sign. Write a paragraph that describes the kind of job you are looking for.

- What services can you perform?
- What experience do you have?
- What kind of worker are you? (What are your work habits?)
- Why should someone hire you?

Make your paragraph at least forty words long.

_____

_____

_____

_____

_____

_____

_____

_____

_____

_____

_____

_____

_____

_____

_____

Pretend your family needs help saving money. Write a paragraph that tells how you could help your family be thrifty.

- What is the difference between a need and a luxury?
- What are your needs?
- What are your luxuries?
- What might you give up?

Make your paragraph at least fifty words long.

_____

_____

_____

_____

_____

_____

_____

_____

_____

_____

_____

_____

_____

_____

_____

_____

_____

Lesson 30, Item 49   Score _____/3   Name _____

Hundreds of years ago, apprentices started at a young age to learn a specific trade at which they earned their living for the rest of their lives. Write an essay comparing an apprentice's education with a modern education.

- What did apprentices learn?
- How did apprentices learn?
- Why was this a practical way of life for people back then?
- What do students of today learn?
- How do students of today learn?
- Why is it necessary to have a more rounded education in the twenty-first century?

Make your essay at least fifty words long.

_____

_____

_____

_____

_____

_____

_____

_____

_____

_____

_____

_____

_____

_____

_____

_____

If you could live anywhere in the world, where would it be? Write an essay describing the perfect place to live.

- Is it a city or a wilderness?
- What plants and animals are there?
- What activities are available?
- How is it different from the London of Sara Crewe's story?

Make your essay at least fifty words long.

_____

_____

_____

_____

_____

_____

_____

_____

_____

_____

_____

_____

_____

_____

_____

_____

_____

If you could help people as Sara Crewe did at the end of the story, whom would you help? Write an essay about how you plan to help others.

- How could you find out who needs help?
- Why would you help them?
- What help would you give?

Make your essay at least sixty words long.

_____

_____

_____

_____

_____

_____

_____

_____

_____

_____

_____

_____

_____

_____

_____

_____

_____

Sylvia, in "A White Heron," was fond of animals. Write a poem about an animal. Use the following questions for ideas.

- What does the animal look like?
- What sounds does it make?
- What does it eat?
- How does it behave?
- If you can touch it, how does it feel?

Make your poem at least ten lines long. Try to make the lines rhyme.

_____

_____

_____

_____

_____

_____

_____

_____

_____

_____

_____

_____

_____

_____

_____

Pretend you are Joe Díaz and want to ask Pete why he took your father's safe and to tell Pete that taking the safe was wrong. Write the conversation you would have with Pete. Write both his words and your words.

- How will you try to convince Pete?
- What reasons will Pete give for taking the safe?

Make your conversation at least seventy words long.

_____

_____

_____

_____

_____

_____

_____

_____

_____

_____

_____

_____

_____

_____

_____

_____

_____

_____

_____

Lesson 80, Item 25   Score ____ /3   Name _____

Pretend you are Harriet Tubman giving advice to Demeter about rescuing Persephone. Write an essay describing a plan you might have suggested.

- What trickery or brave deed might you suggest to Demeter?
- How might Demeter use your suggestion to rescue Persephone?
- How will the whole plan work?

Make your essay at least seventy words long.

_____

Of the different periods of time described so far in your textbooks, in which period would you like to have lived? Write an essay describing the type of house you would live in, what you would eat, and your occupation or schooling.

- Why would you like this life?
- What things would you not like?

Make your essay at least seventy words long.

_____

_____

_____

_____

_____

_____

_____

_____

_____

_____

_____

_____

_____

_____

_____

_____

_____

Sara Crewe and Huck Finn were alike in some ways but different in others. Write an essay telling how their lives were alike and how they were different.

- How were their hardships similar?
- How were their families different?
- How were the endings of their stories alike?

Make your essay at least eighty words long.

_____

_____

_____

_____

_____

_____

_____

_____

_____

_____

_____

_____

_____

_____

_____

_____

_____

Tom felt he had done something noble by taking Becky's punishment for tearing the teacher's book. Write an essay telling about a noble deed you have done.

- What was your noble deed?
- Why did you do your noble deed?
- Why do you think your deed was noble?
- How did you feel afterward?

Make your essay at least eighty words long.

_____

_____

_____

_____

_____

_____

_____

_____

_____

_____

_____

_____

_____

_____

_____

_____

_____

_____

Write a story about two people who are lost in a forest. Try to answer the following questions.

- What does the forest look and sound like?
- What dangers and problems do they encounter?
- How do they overcome them?
- What do they fear?
- How do they conquer their fears?
- How will they get help?

Make your story at least one hundred words long.

_____

_____

_____

_____

_____

_____

_____

_____

_____

_____

_____

_____

_____

_____

_____

_____

Guidelines for Evaluating Writing Items

General Guidelines

Did the student

- indent paragraphs?
- write in complete sentences?
- begin each sentence with a capital letter and end it with appropriate punctuation?
- spell most words correctly?
- stick to the subject?
- answer the questions or follow the directions in the prompt?

Scoring

If you wish to score the writing items, use the general guidelines listed above along with the following scoring guide:

0 The student wrote nothing.
1 The student wrote something but did not answer any of the questions or respond to any of the issues raised in the prompt.
2 The student answered some of the questions and responded to some of the issues raised in the prompt.
3 The student answered all the questions and responded to all the issues raised in the prompt.

Specific Guidelines

Lesson 10, Item 17

Did the student answer the following questions in the prompt?

- What services can you perform?
- What experience do you have?
- What kind of worker are you? (What are your work habits?)
- Why should someone hire you?

Did the student write at least forty words?

Lesson 20, Item 17

Did the student answer the following questions in the prompt?

- What is the difference between a need and a luxury?
- What are your needs?
- What are your luxuries?
- What might you give up?

Did the student write at least fifty words?

Lesson 30, Item 49

Did the student answer the following questions in the prompt?

- What did apprentices learn?
- How did apprentices learn?
- Why was this a practical way of life for people back then?
- What do students of today learn?
- How do students of today learn?
- Why is it necessary to have a more rounded education in the twenty-first century?

Did the student write at least fifty words?

Lesson 40, Item 18

Did the student answer the following questions in the prompt?

- Is it a city or a wilderness?
- What plants and animals are there?
- What activities are available?
- How is it different from the London of Sara Crewe's story?

Did the student write at least fifty words?

Lesson 50, Item 18

Did the student answer the following questions in the prompt?

- How could you find out who needs help?
- Why would you help them?
- What help would you give?

Did the student write at least sixty words?

Lesson 60, Item 54

Did the student write a poem answering some of the following questions in the prompt?

- What does the animal look like?
- What sounds does it make?
- What does it eat?
- How does it behave?
- If you can touch it, how does it feel?

Did the student write at least ten lines? Do the lines rhyme?

Lesson 70, Item 24

Did the student respond appropriately to the prompt and answer the following questions as part of the conversation?

- How will you try to convince Pete?
- What reasons will Pete give for taking the safe?

Did the student write at least seventy words?

Lesson 80, Item 25

Did the student answer the following questions in the prompt?

- What trickery or brave deed might you suggest to Demeter?
- How might Demeter use your suggestion to rescue Persephone?
- How will the whole plan work?

Did the student write at least seventy words?

Lesson 90, Item 54

Did the student respond appropriately to the prompt and answer the following questions?

- Why would you like this life?
- What things would you not like?

Did the student write at least seventy words?

Lesson 100, Item 24

Did the student answer the following questions in the prompt?

- How were their hardships similar?
- How were their families different?
- How were the endings of their stories alike?

Did the student write at least eighty words?

Lesson 110, Item 25

Did the student answer the following questions in the prompt?

- What was your noble deed?
- Why did you do your noble deed?
- Why do you think your deed was noble?
- How did you feel afterward?

Did the student write at least eighty words?

Lesson 120, Item 50

Did the student answer the following questions in the prompt?

- What does the forest look and sound like?
- What dangers and problems do they encounter?
- How do they overcome them?
- What do they fear?
- How do they conquer their fears?
- How will they get help?

Did the student write at least one hundred words?